HILL ABLAZE

HILL ABLAZE

by

Bill Butler
one of the team at the heart of the East African revival

HODDER AND STOUGHTON
LONDON SYDNEY AUCKLAND TORONTO

Foreword

Hill Ablaze is a true story and for that reason contains much of failure, coldness and sin. It is also a story of forgiveness, grace and love, and of the power of the Blood of Jesus Christ to cleanse, and where He cleanses to fill with His Holy Spirit.

My thanks to all in the Ruanda office who combined to make this book possible, to Joy Cathcart and Marie Walters who typed it, and to my wife and family who encouraged me to write it in the first place. Most of all my love and gratitude to all my brethren in East Africa from whom and with whom my wife and I have learned and are still learning such deep lessons in God's school of revival. To them this book is dedicated.

BILL BUTLER

Introduction

by His Grace the Most Reverend Erica Sabiti, until recently Archbishop of the Province of Uganda, Rwanda, Burundi and Boga-Zaire.

IT GIVES ME great joy to write a brief introduction to this book written by Canon Bill Butler.

Bill was a missionary in Uganda for twenty-four years and is now General Secretary of the Ruanda (C.M.S.) Mission. He and his wife Nancy are members of a team raised up by God, of Africans and Europeans who, like Moses, caught a vision of His holy fire burning, not consuming—the burning fire of His love! Before Moses could be used by God to deliver His captive people, he had first to hear God say to him "put off your shoes from off your feet, for the place on which you stand is holy ground". He needed cleansing and forgiveness and a right relationship with a holy God before he could be used as an instrument of blessing to others.

Bill and Nancy had to learn the same costly lesson, that before ever God could use them as He longed to do, they must experience in their own lives the continual cleansing power of His precious blood and the fullness of His Holy Spirit.

This is the story told with moving frankness and simplicity of God's dealings with them in Africa over many years. It is not a success story, but it rings true, and warms my own heart as I read it.

I hesitated when first invited to write this introduction feeling that this book deserved somebody better known and more widely recognised to commend it. I have one qualification, however, the fact that I was myself part of the "Hill Ablaze" of which the concluding chapters tell.

I recommend this book with all my heart, praying that all who read it may discover as did the two disciples on the Emmaus Road the secret of a burning heart—"Jesus Himself drew near and went with them ... did not our hearts burn within us while He talked to us on the road, while He opened to us the scriptures" (Luke 24:15, 32).

ERICA SABITI

I

It was a hot sticky morning at Mukono when Yokana burst in at my study door. If I'd seen him coming I'd have slammed it in his face, so angry and frustrated had I become with him and his fellow theological students. They brought out the worst in me. They seemed so indecently happy, with no sense of shame; the way they spoke of Jesus and the sins from which they claimed He had so marvellously delivered them. No wonder they were known throughout the College as "balokole"—the saved ones—and hardly surprising that they were so unpopular.

"Bwana, do go into Kampala this afternoon; there's a lady missionary staying there from Ruanda; she's on fire; I am sure she can help you!" What cheek! As if *I* needed help—from a fiery female at that—let alone one from Ruanda. Of course, many of my friends were missionaries there, but since being ordained and located to Bishop Tucker College, Mukono, in Uganda, I had come to look at things a little differently. These conservative evangelicals really were rather narrow after all, and all their talk about revival did get a bit on one's nerves. On the other hand I often felt pretty miserable and not completely at home in the set-up in which I now found myself. Perhaps she would be able to advise me as to how one got accepted by these balokole.

With mixed motives and considerable reluctance I found myself taking Yokana's advice, and driving my old jalopy the fifteen miles or so to Kampala, where the "lady missionary from Ruanda" was staying. I had never met her before, although, of course, I had heard about her, but as soon as we met I sensed something in her which made me both resentful and wistful. If only I could unburden myself to her; explain the sort of person I really was; and how these saved Africans didn't understand or appreciate me! She listened patiently and attentively to all I had to say, without trying to excuse or vindicate her own position. For a moment there was silence; then she gave perhaps the straightest look a European had ever given me. "You know, I can't help wondering if you have ever been broken?" she said. It was like a kick from a mule!—so completely unexpected and totally unfair.

Then, out of the blue, almost as if I heard them spoken aloud came the words of Psalm 51; verse 17, "The sacrifices of God are a broken spirit, a broken and a contrite heart Thou will not despise". It was as though quite suddenly, almost blindingly, I saw myself as Jesus saw me, as I *really* was. My pride, my rebellion, my unwillingness to let go the failures and secret sins that for years had held me; so reluctant to allow anyone, least of all Africans, to pierce my British reserve: that mask behind which I had been trying with so little success to hide. Then came another verse, one I had heard again and again, but now as though for the first time, "This is My body ... broken for you; My blood ... shed for you." I looked back on two miserable years of defeat and failure and despair.

It didn't require two weeks, or even two hours; in the

end it took scarcely two minutes to come to the point where I was willing for Jesus to have His way and begin to break me. It was all surprisingly unemotional. There wasn't even time to pray together before my friend's hostess came bustling in to offer us a cup of tea. But deep down I knew I had crossed the Rubicon from which there could be no turning back.

Although it is now over thirty years since allowing that first crack in the iceberg, and there have had to be many subsequent times of breaking and melting, the cycle of renewed fullness and blessing has always followed repentance and cleansing.

I returned to Mukono that evening in a daze, not knowing what was going to happen, but with a deep sense of peace; conscious that now "the government was on His shoulder". The responsibility was no longer mine but His, and all I had to do was obey.

Next morning the Lord woke me early after a sound night's sleep (I had been sleeping very badly), and for the first time for months my "quiet time" really came alive. "If you are offering your gift at the altar, and there remember that your brother has something against you, leave your gift before the altar and go; first be reconciled to your brother, then come and offer your gift" (Matthew 5 : 23). If ever there was a brother with whom I needed to be reconciled, and whose forgiveness I needed to ask, it was William Nagenda, later to be known as an evangelist of world-wide repute. He, like Yokana and one or two others, had been aware of my growing coldness, my compromise with liberal theology, and general spiritual malaise, and had lovingly expressed concern from time to time; even to my chagrin assuring me that he was praying for me! William had been especially anxious about me, a fact which in my wretched pride I had bitterly resented and shown in many ways. This was the first real test of "brokenness"—the willingness to be humbled, to take the way of the Cross, to admit my failure specifically to another and ask his forgiveness for the wrong I had done him.

It was not easy, and all sorts of excuses came to mind. William might be away from home—it was his vacation—it was unseemly for a European to acknowledge that he had been in the wrong, especially to one of his students (shades of Colonial days). It would be harmful for William's pride (to which the obvious answer came that it would be very good for mine)—but once more I cranked up my old 1928 Hillman and drove the thirty-five miles to where William was staying. I'll never forget that journey! It was as if there were two passengers in the car with me. One reminding me of the loss of face and prestige that was bound to ensue, the Other that this in a very practical and specific way was what "dying to self" was all about. Paul was able joyfully to exclaim, "I am crucified with Christ, nevertheless I live, yet not I" (that old self-centred egotistical "I" crossed out at Calvary) "but Christ liveth in me . . ." Dr. Joe Church, in his little motto card familiar to many, shows within the "I" a proud, stiff-necked little man, standing erect and resistant to the claims of his Lord. In the curve of the "C", the same man is seen kneeling, penitent, broken, as he prays:

Lord bend this proud and stiff-necked "I",
Help me to bow the neck and die
Beholding Him on Calvary,
Who bowed His head for me.

In that first kindergarten step of faith and obedience, so simple and yet so costly, I began to taste afresh the wonder of Christ's love and forgiveness. As I drew up at the small house where William and Sala were spending their holiday, and tooted the horn, they came running out. Before I could say a word William took one look at my face, and with an indescribable look of joy greeted me, "Praise the Lord, brother!" My prepared speech, like that of the penitent prodigal, was brushed aside, as William hugged me as I had never been hugged before, in an African embrace. For the first time in two years I knew myself one with an African! That faltering step was the first of many. Never before had I known such readiness to forgive or such warmth of love—God's love, Calvary love—as met me then. It was just like coming home! I found myself immediately part of a warm praising fellowship I had never dreamed of or experienced, in which one was safe; accepted without any need for pretence, but a fellowship which would challenge fearlessly, ruthlessly, yet with amazing grace anything less than "the highest"! Nor, in their wisdom and love, did the Africans deal with me as so many would have done in England. When somebody is converted or blessed, or takes a new step forward spiritually, our tendency is to say, "Splendid, now we can leave them to it!"—but not so with these Spirit-taught men. Indeed their reaction was, "Praise God, Bill's had a blessing, now we can really get to work on him!"—and that, with remarkable insight and grace, is just what they did.

Many were the lessons taught in that school of revival which, had it not been for the faithfulness and discernment of my African brethren, I would never have learned.

Those "wretched balokole" whom I had so resented and feared became, overnight, my brethren to whom, under God, I owe an immense debt of love.

2

MY FATHER GAVE up a prosperous business career in his early thirties to go out to India as a Secretary of the British and Foreign Bible Society. He became engaged to my mother at the Keswick Convention just before sailing, and she joined him in Madras for their wedding a few months later. On their first leave in England I was born, a Caesarean baby, and their only child, on the eve of World War I, which was actually declared while we were on our way back to Allahabad in North India.

I have vivid memories of the Bible House at Allahabad; a rather ornate building, with offices and stores downstairs, and our own comfortable quarters surrounded by wide verandahs on the upper floor. Even missionaries were part of the "British Raj" in those days, and expected to live in some style, and we had the usual quota of servants, including my own bearer, Nunkoo. I recollect a carriage and pair which took us to the park in the cool of the evening, just before sunset, to hear the band playing. I remember, too, my godfather Uncle Roddy (R. T. Archibald, father of the Children's Special Service Mission and Scripture Union in Southern India) who was a great favourite with all children. Best of all I have the happiest memories of my father, sitting on the chintz-covered sofa in our drawing room, telling me fascinating Bible stories. There were other moments, like the time when I deliberately jumped on his new patent leather shoes to see what would happen. I soon discovered! But that was the only occasion I ever remember him spanking me. My mother, on the other hand, determined not to spoil her only child, quite frequently had recourse to the back of a hairbrush when I had been particularly naughty. I don't think it did me any harm, and I certainly had the greatest love and affection for her, as well as a healthy respect for her wristy follow-through!

Those were halcyon days. The sweet sticky flavour of "jalabies", fly-blown contraband occasionally smuggled to me past my mother's watchful eye by indulgent servants! The rockets soaring up and up into the sky (father loved fireworks and delighted to let them off at the slightest pretext—what better than Armistice Day 1918?), and then the "oohs" and "aahs" of wonder as the brightly-coloured stars descended! The blaze of lights with which the Bible House was illuminated on special occasions; hundreds of tiny pots of oil with floating wicks strung together in a glittering chain. One less happy, but equally vivid, recollection is that of a walk with my father along the banks of the Ganges, where to my astonishment I saw an old man lying on a bed of spikes. On asking how long he had lain there, we were told thirty years. "Why?" I asked, struck by his sad expression. Father explained that the poor man was doing it in order, as he hoped, to obtain forgiveness of his sins. The whole episode must have made a marked impression on me, for I can still recall it clearly, as also my child-like comment, "But Daddy, hasn't anybody ever told him about Jesus?"

Nor will I ever forget my first breathtaking glimpse of the Himalayas, on one of our periodic trips up to the hill station in Landour, with the "Khud", a seemingly bottomless abyss on one side, and the snow-tipped mountain peaks soaring up to the clouds on the other. Poor father, left alone down in the plains in the sweltering heat of an Indian summer! What delightful letters he used to write, with fascinating little pin men sketches in the margin! And what excitement when at last he could join us, and we were once again united.

My mother and I returned to England ahead of him for furlough soon after the war ended; a trip which may well have accounted for some of her prematurely grey hairs, for from her accounts and my own recollections, it was quite a lively journey. On one hair-raising occasion my mother went to our cabin where she had left me asleep, to find an empty bunk. I was discovered sitting on the knee of a singularly villainous-looking "lascar", in a circle of equally disreputable comrades, telling them the Bible stories my father had so memorably imparted to me. Another time, I was found liberally sprinkling the other children on board ship with the deck hose. The captain himself came to the rescue and, holding me by the soaking seat of my trousers, returned me to my mother saying, "Madam, I believe this is your property?"

We eventually found ourselves in the beautiful Sussex village of Broadwater where at the age of six, on March 31st, 1921, I gave my heart to the Lord Jesus. One Sunday evening mother had been reading aloud—I think for the fourth time—one of Amy le Feuvre's unforgettable children's books, *Teddy's Button*. She had reached the point at which Teddy, the son of a soldier father killed in battle, himself "enlisted" under Jesus's banner as a soldier in His army. I had known about Jesus, of course, from my earliest days, and loved what I knew. I could see how much He meant to my parents, who in a very real sense introduced me to Him as a living, loving Saviour, but that night I myself entered into a personal relationship with Him, though, of course, this new relationship had to grow and be worked out at each successive stage of development. I walked down the village street singing at the top of my voice:

Joy, joy, joy, with joy my heart is ringing,
Joy, joy, joy, His love to me is known;
My sins are all forgiven, I'm on my way to Heaven,
My heart is bubbling over with His joy, joy, joy.

In parenthesis may I add an incident for the encouragement of those who work among young children. Visiting little Rachel, the daughter of missionary friends, when she was lying ill in Mengo Hospital in Kampala, I asked how old she was. When she replied that she was six I said, "That's a lovely age to be; I was six when I gave my heart to Jesus." Quick as a flash Rachel retorted, "I was two and a half!" Sure enough, it transpired that as she was being put to bed one night by her mother, Rachel looked up and asked, "Where does Jesus live, mummy?" "In heaven", was the reply, "but He loves to live in people's hearts, if they will only ask Him in." Straight away that little girl, now a missionary herself and mother of four children, invited Jesus into her heart. I thank God for my own early encounter with the Lord, and for the pitfalls from which He preserved me as a result.

The following year saw me at Monkton Combe Junior School near Bath. A photograph taken at that time shows a rather solemn small boy of seven with freckles on his nose and a very tight Eton jacket. The separation from my parents wasn't easy, and it proved to be the last time I saw my father. He died of peritonitis a year later, aged forty-two. The time at Monkton was brief and not entirely happy. Much of this was doubtless my own fault, for I was rather a precocious child, and like many missionaries' children missed my parents acutely. Holidays however were an entirely different matter, being spent in the hospitable home of Nella Allen, a lifelong friend of my mother's, who welcomed me into her home as one of her own family.

In God's perfect timing, though then it seemed mysterious that my father should die so young, He brought my mother home to England just when she was needed. Only a few months later I collapsed with rheumatic fever which laid me on my back for the next two years. It was a testing time for my mother, herself far from strong, desperately missing my father, and possessing little of this world's goods, but she had an implicit faith in her Heavenly Father. Friends were kind; none more so than the two maiden sisters who owned Mayfield Farm near Monkton Junior School, where we stayed throughout my illness, and where my mother nursed me back to health.

We were drawn very close together during that time, and remained so for as long as she lived. She supplemented her meagre income with paintings and artwork (she was a gifted artist), and I never once heard her grumble or complain. The doctor who attended me throughout my long illness lived two or three miles away in Bath. He not only visited me every day, but for three months when I was critically ill admitted me to his nursing home. When all was over he refused to accept any payment, simply saying to my mother, "You are a Christian—give me the credit for being a Christian too." Soon after this a generous grant from the British and Foreign Bible Society made it possible for us to buy a small bungalow in Pagham, near Bognor, an ideal place in which to recuperate. This, in summer, proved a sound investment, as we were able to let it to holiday-makers, camping out ourselves in the adjoining garage. We appropriately named our new home "Allahabad", although anything less like the palatial Bible House in India could hardly be imagined. However, it was home again, for which we were grateful, and we were able to share it with many friends in need of a seaside holiday.

After recovering from my long illness, I was fortunate enough to receive a "Presentation" from a generous Governor to Christ's Hospital, known to the uninitiated as "The Blue Coat School".

When just thirteen years old, I spent a holiday at Paignton, enjoying my first experience of a C.S.S.M. Houseparty. My aunt was leader of the lady workers, with Geoffrey Rogers, later one of the founders of Lee Abbey, as the men's leader. I was in the party as a privileged mascot! One Sunday afternoon, resplendent in blue coat, complete with bands, buttons, yellow stockings and knee-breeches, I wandered down to the harbour to look at the fishing boats. I noticed a group of small boys looking curiously at me and whispering, but loftily ignored them, until at last one of them could endure it no longer and burst out, "Are you a boy or a gal?" (I didn't mind! I was really quite proud of my uniform and even prouder in later years to see it on my son.) I was devastated, however, by the youngster's reply, when having learned that it was my school uniform he exclaimed, "Sloppy boy!"

That August at Paignton proved a momentous month. On missionary day I was given a lift to the beach in the sidecar of a young recently qualified doctor, who was travelling round the coast on his motorbike visiting every C.S.S.M., and recruiting prayer partners for the recently founded Ruanda Mission (C.M.S.). His name was Joe Church. It was my first meeting with one who later made a great impact on me, becoming one of my closest friends. I was impressed by talking to a genuine missionary recruit, and shyly confided to him that since my father's death God had been calling me to be a missionary. Joe's answer was typical, "If God means you to serve Him abroad, you will. Perhaps we'll meet in Africa one day!" It was a prophetic utterance.

Although I had attended several beach services in previous years it was never from the inside, and that month I saw that I had grown slack in my spiritual life. Prayer and Bible study had been neglected, and I began to realise that if ever I was to be of use abroad, I must first learn how to serve God at home. It was a great encouragement to meet another boy from Christ's Hospital at Paignton. He was senior to me, but we were drawn together, and began to talk and pray over the possibility of starting a Christian Union at "Housey" as we called our school. He knew two or three other Christians whom he thought would appreciate such a venture. The following term we approached the Head, later Sir Hamilton Fyfe, a great and wise Headmaster, and asked his permission to meet. This he willingly granted. A few weeks later Mr. Vereker, Secretary of the Crusaders' Union, came to speak at the inaugural meeting of our Christian Union. We managed to recruit quite a few to that opening session and, by God's grace, in spite of many ups and downs the C.U. has gone on ever since. Thrilled as we were with the launching of the Christian Union, I knew I had never won anyone for the Lord; and if He really meant as much to me as I professed, then surely I ought to tell others what He had done for me. But I didn't want to be laughed at or thought peculiar. I began to pray for my friend, Philip. One half holiday, we had been taken to the tuck shop by an elderly relative and given a magnificent tea. As a result we were excused attendance at Hall and were on our own. I'm not sure what I said to him, but I can remember my knees wobbling and my mouth drying up! To my astonishment Philip thanked me and said he had been longing to know how to become a Christian! Then and there we knelt and he gave his heart to the Lord, and I tasted for the first time the joy of seeing somebody born again before my eyes. Several others became Christians that term, and the C.U. doubled its membership, but nothing ever quite compared with that first friend's conversion.

On the whole, I was very happy at Christ's Hospital and greatly enjoyed the six years I spent there. Situated near Horsham, in one of the loveliest parts of Sussex, surrounded by acres of its own grounds, playing fields and farms, its mellow red-brick buildings, gracious quadrangles and sweeping avenues, lend it an almost story-book quality. The school's long association with the City of London, and the Lord Mayor who annually visits and is visited by the school, make for a sense of history and continuity with the past, as do many famous "old Blues" whose names linger on in the houses now called after them: Coleridge, Lamb, Middleton and Peele, to name but a few. Admittedly it boasts (or did boast) a somewhat spartan régime. We slept on horsehair mattresses supported by boards, and the food was wholesome rather than toothsome, but the tone was excellent and bullying virtually unknown. The Chapel services were simple and dignified, and the singing and music, under the inspiring leadership of Dr. Laing, made a lasting impression, as did the famous Brangwyn pictures on the Chapel walls. If the sermons were not startling, at least the pictures were.

The next two summer holidays I was privileged to spend at West Runton Camp, where I met a certain Dick Rees, and with a group of other youngsters joined in praying fervently for the conversion of his tough young brother, Tom. My mother, prayerful woman that she was, joined her petition to ours. It was hardly surprising, therefore, the following term to receive a terse postcard from Dick, "Tom saved, Hallelujah!"

Although I played rugger and ran for my House, I can claim no academic distinction at Christ's Hospital. This was due in some measure to my own laziness and lack of effort, and partly to the fact that I had lost two important years of schooling through rheumatic fever. The only prizes I remember winning were for English, Reading and Scripture. My grasp of mathematics was abysmal and hardly improved by my maths master who used to assure me, "You're a fool, Butler, a fool. What are you, boy?" to which I could only reply, "A fool, sir!" The Headmaster, sympathising with my sense of vocation to Christian service, offered me two extra years to catch up lost time and try for University entrance. But I was eager to support my mother as quickly as possible and this, coupled with my lack of enthusiasm for study, led me to accept a job when still not quite seventeen years old at the London Fruit Exchange.

3

DURING MY LAST year at Christ's Hospital, we sold our little bungalow at Pagham Beach, and bought a semi-detached house in West Croydon. This move had far-reaching consequences.

I have sometimes described the following period as two years in Covent Garden learning what fruit looked like, and four years in the London Fruit Exchange at Spitalfields learning how to sell it. Also, as doing my first language study at Covent Garden, which I have been trying to forget ever since! It was a tough life, and unlike anything I had known. Later, I came to realise that this, too, was part of God's preparation for the work He had in store for me, though at the time I found it distinctly irksome. It was a great thrill to take home my first weekly pay packet of eighteen shillings and sixpence, of which five shillings went on fares and five shillings for lunches, the rest being handed over to my mother. We made ends meet by letting our two spare rooms. One lodger was the Rev. Bill Bailey, curate to Clifford Martin, vicar of Christ Church, Croydon, both of whom became very good friends. The latter in due course was made Bishop of Liverpool, and years later ordained me priest at St. Helen's, Lancashire, where Canon Bailey—as he had then become—was Vicar.

Looking back on this period, it is easy to see what

opportunities were missed, and how much more literally fruitful that time could have been for the Lord. Much of my witness in the firm for which I worked was negative. I didn't drink, I didn't smoke, I didn't swear—but neither did I do anything very positive, at least in business hours! Paul's advice to Timothy, "Whatsoever your hand finds to do, do it with all your might," had not yet registered. How I wish now, for instance, that I had used that time to attend evening classes for shorthand, typing and book-keeping, skills which would later have proved invaluable.

There was much activity outside the office, and it was easy enough to convince myself that it was all for the Lord, but those hours spent rushing madly from one meeting to another were often unguided, although there was a genuine desire to know God better, and to serve Him more worthily. There were sporadic attempts to "bring under the body" and "master the flesh", sometimes for months on end, when I would rise at six o'clock, go for a mile run and have a cold bath, only to fall sound asleep at my bedside when it came to that all important encounter with God. Every Friday evening along with hundreds of others I would crowd into Westminster Chapel to hear Dr. Campbell Morgan. Deep down, though, I knew I was a defeated Christian. Defeated in my thinking, defeated by indiscipline, defeated by habits. Paul's heartcry of Romans 7, verse 15, found an echo, "I do not do what I want to, but I do the very thing I hate ... I can will what is right but I cannot do it ... wretched man that I am, who will deliver me from this body of death?" I was still unable to go on and say with Paul, "Thanks be to God through Jesus Christ our Lord." I appeared a cheerful enough youngster, with many friends, few of whom suspected the inner struggles which were going on. Christ Church, Croydon, was a live evangelical church; Clifford Martin an outstanding Vicar; and our Mission church, St. Christopher's, built in the adjoining new housing area, with the Rev. Aubrey Evan Hopkins as curate-in-charge, saw to it that we were rarely idle! Throughout those six years I was engaged in various forms of active Christian service: parish visiting and magazine distribution; Sunday School teaching; helping to run a Scout group; later assisting with a boys' club and camps; public house visiting late on Saturday nights. My mother hardly saw anything of me and when she ventured gently to remonstrate, her well-meant efforts were seldom appreciated.

There were lighter moments. The lady I visited on the new estate who was so reluctant to tell me what her husband did for a living; eventually divulging rather coyly that "'e was a night gardener". On my next visit I found that he had been arrested and charged with housebreaking and sentenced to six months' hard labour! Or the hard-working mum who proudly reported that "'er son Frankie what 'ad gorn to Borstal had just been made a prefec'"! No mother could have been prouder of an Etonian son. There were also the open-air meetings on the site of St. Christopher's where, whatever our hearers may have thought, we at least gained useful experience.

She really was attractive, with a bright, sunny smile, and a twinkle in her eye that argued a sense of humour. She wore a Crusader badge and had evidently noticed mine, for she nodded across from the opposite platform, and what could I do but nod back? She was on the down train platform and I was on the London side, and for several weeks we smiled and nodded at each other every morning. It was rather fun. While quite liking girls I had not had very much to do with them; a childhood without brothers and sisters, and the somewhat monastic background of a public school, hadn't given me much opportunity. I remembered Bishop Taylor Smith's words however, in his sonorous booming voice, addressing a young people's meeting, "Young man, young woman, you are never too young to begin to pray for the partner of God's choice!" That struck me as sound advice and still does. So, although I was only about eighteen, I had begun to pray that in His own time, God would lead me to the partner of His choice. There were one or two girls I had met, and wondered . . . might this be the one? . . . The bright-eyed lass across the platform, for instance?

Meanwhile our energetic curate often used to bemoan the fact that it was impossible for "the Misses Wyse" to attend our weekly young people's meeting. I don't know why, but somehow I had a vivid mental picture of them as a couple of little old spinsters and could never quite see how they would fit in with a group of youngsters like ourselves. Until one day, at a church function, I met "the Misses Wyse" in person. One of them was my lady of the platform. The other was her young sister Nancy—and it didn't take long to discover that here for me was the "partner of God's choice"! It really was love at first sight. But the course of true love certainly didn't run all that smoothly. Nancy was the youngest of five attractive daughters. Two brothers and a sister had previously died. She had gained a fund of sound common sense from her Scottish parents and was not going to be rushed into any sort of involvement without being quite sure it was God's will for her.

Brought up in a thoroughly God-fearing tradition with hymn singing round the piano on Sunday evenings and any amount of care and concern for the poor and needy, she had only recently come to know Christ as her Saviour, and wanted to be very sure before committing herself to me or to anyone else.

Nancy's conversion was a gradual process rather than a sudden crisis, and she found it difficult to state any specific date on which she became a Christian. One of her sisters persuaded her to go along to Crusaders, and although at first she was rather a thorn in the flesh to her leaders—and on one occasion at least had to be asked to leave for misbehaviour—it left a deep impression on her. At the same time she was attending confirmation classes conducted by Clifford Martin which also influenced her. Perhaps the most decisive episode was when a senior member of the Crusader class told how God had guided her regarding a job when she left school. This challenged Nancy and helped her to realise for the first time that God had a plan for her life as well. Later, she qualified as a dispenser, working long hours for three doctors, and spending almost all her spare time in a non-stop round of parish visiting, Sunday School and similar activities at St. Christopher's, much as I was doing. Inevitably we saw a good deal of each other; the more I saw of her, the more firmly convinced I became that here indeed was my future partner, but how and when?

As an only child with a strong sense of obligation to assist my widowed mother, I did not feel able to contemplate marriage for some time. Nancy, too, although the youngest of a fairly large family, felt she must take her share in nursing her father who, following a severe stroke, was an invalid for seven years. There was yet another question mark over our future. I made no secret of the fact that I believed God had called me to serve Him one day overseas and Nancy, while sympathetic to my call and herself definitely interested in the possibility of missionary service, was by no means certain that God was calling her to be a missionary's wife. In spite of these tensions, our friendship continued to deepen and mature. Most Thursdays we would join a party of friends from the local Crusader Fellowship at Purley Ice Rink. Those were hilarious evenings; and though neither of us became outstanding skaters, we achieved a reasonable enough standard to enjoy ourselves and unwind a little from our other hectic activities.

Never strong physically, from Nancy flowed from the earliest days a strength of character and tenacity of purpose, doubtless inherited from her Scottish forbears, which stood us in good stead in later years.

4

Of course I had heard of the Missionary Training Colony. "The Colony, where men were men, and women were only in the way!" The Colony which had produced such missionary heroes as Fenton Hall, "The Three Freds", Leonard Harris, Horace Banner and others. I had heard of its spartan fare, its army huts, camp beds and iron discipline. I had heard, too, of the vision that had inspired its founder and leader, Captain Godfrey Buxton, whose brother Alfred had left Cambridge and gone out to the Congo to join the famous C. T. Studd, returning later to England to urge his brother Godfrey to train men for similar pioneer situations for which no amount of academic training could ever fit them. I had heard, too, something of the way in which that vision had been fulfilled; the little wooden "Colony" of army huts that had miraculously materialised in the midst of suburban Upper Norwood. And of the faith basis on which it was run, looking for all material provision only to the Lord. I had once attended as a guest for a weekend there and, while enormously impressed by all I saw, and by those I met, had firmly decided that wherever else the Lord might lead me for training, it must certainly never be there! Which perhaps is why in March 1937 I found myself trudging down the curving cinder path which led to the Missionary Training Colony.

Events had moved rapidly the previous year. An unforgettable visit to the Keswick Convention had convinced me that it would not be long before I got my marching orders. A kind friend made it possible for me to attend with the E.U.S.A. Houseparty (Evangelical Union of South America). Under the inspiring leadership of Stuart McNairn, and sharing a room with Charles Glass (himself a product of the Colony), I began to wonder if South America might not be my mission field. True, I had always assumed that it would be India, but realised that God might well direct me elsewhere. I was strongly attracted by Stuart McNairn's warmth and humanity, and by his delightful sense of humour and obvious spirituality, and liked immensely all that I saw of others in the E.U.S.A. fellowship. At the Friday missionary meeting, I stood to rededicate myself for whatever the Lord might require of me. I returned home bubbling with enthusiasm to share it all with Nancy and my mother, to whom it must have brought back many memories.

A few months later an uncle, who made little Christian profession but had a soft spot for his sister—my mother—paid a visit to England from South Africa where he operated a flourishing legal practice. One day he made the startling pronouncement that in view of the fact that sooner or later I would probably be following the example set by my father in offering for some form of full-time service, he proposed to settle an annual sum of money on my mother which would render her reasonably independent for life! This generous offer, so unexpected, was surely God's provision. A few weeks later I went to see Stuart McNairn to ask his advice regarding training, and heard with little surprise that he recommended the Colony.

One knotty problem still remained—was Nancy sufficiently clear regarding her own call to the mission field? Did she love me enough to marry me? Until these issues were resolved, how right was it to continue with our existing relationship? Godfrey Buxton's unequivocal advice, on being consulted, was to make a clean break and not see each other during the two years I was at the Colony! It was an agonising decision to make, but after much prayer and heart-searching we both agreed it was the right thing to do. It involved resigning from all the activities at Christ Church and St. Christopher's, which I had previously hoped might be maintained from the Colony only three miles away. It meant, too, difficult explanations to Nancy's parents and others.

During the weeks that elapsed before I started at the Colony, the doubts and fears that had loomed so large in Nancy's mind were gradually dispelled. She became assured that God was calling her to service overseas and, too, that we were meant for each other! Strangely enough it did not occur to either of us that this had in any way altered the situation! We parted, as planned, and a very costly parting it was, fully expecting not to see each other again for two years when, God willing, we would become engaged. Judge then our joy when only a day or two after arriving at the Colony, Godfrey Buxton enquired kindly after Nancy and, on being informed of the recent developments, assured me that in view of the very altered circumstances he felt that, far from parting, we should see as much of each other as possible!

Those two years were certainly among the happiest and carefree I have known. "B.G.", as Godfrey Buxton was affectionately known, was a man of integrity and the highest ideals who never expected a standard lower than that which God demands, and who by his unfailing courtesy and uncomplaining courage (living in constant pain from a hip shattered in World War I), set us all a shining example of practical Christianity. His wife, Dorothea, née Reader Harris, was held in equal awe and affection among us with her clarion call "tea, coffee, cocoa?" ringing out on Woodend evenings, when we gathered each week in the Buxtons' gracious drawing room to darn socks and hear letters from various Colony brethren on the field. Other members of staff included Albert Blackwell—"A.V.B." to us all—with his dry humour and penetrating perception; and Commander David Williams, the Camp Adjutant, a disciplinarian and devoted servant of Jesus Christ. There were the visiting speakers and lecturers too; dear old Barclay Buxton, B.G.'s ageing father with his beaming smile and profound love for the Lord and His Word; Percy Faunch, mystic and prophet, speaking sometimes far above the heads of his less saintly hearers; Mr. Chapman, introducing successive generations of Colony men to the skills of saw, plane and lathe. How much we owed to these and many others for the teaching and, even more important, the example they gave us.

Then there were the famous "Russian baths". Baths so cold, at six o'clock in the morning, that we used to "rush in and rush out" of them after a strenuous run or P.T. in the adjoining park.

There were the unhurried quiet times, broken on occasion by muffled snores from some earnest kneeling figure, discovering for himself the truth that the spirit was willing but the flesh weak. There were the meals, prepared and cooked by each of us in turn, at first under

A.V.B.'s or Mrs. Buxton's watchful eye, and later for two weeks on our own; and the unforgettable occasion when one of us, mistaking his tins, made an appetising looking custard out of mustard powder! The practical sessions, too, when we learnt (sometimes disastrously) to cut each other's hair. The shoes we cobbled and subsequently hobbled in, the socks we darned until they could be darned no longer. In the afternoons we explored with varying degrees of success different aspects of building, plumbing and electric wiring, with occasional sessions on car maintenance. Those not so engaged would hoe and weed in the extensive grounds surrounding the Colony. Football matches were arranged with neighbouring rival institutions—Spurgeons, All Nations, even the School for the Blind who not infrequently managed to beat us, especially when the light began to fail.

Living at close quarters with thirty other men provided excellent training for the mission field. We came together from varying backgrounds and nationalities. Ludwig Dewitz had barely escaped from Germany with his life, after it had been discovered that he had Jewish blood. He would attend Bible studies with his Hebrew Old Testament and Greek New Testament and translate freely from them both as we went along. He would electrify an audience by saying, "Dear friends, please excuse my bad language," which always brought the house down! Later he became remarkably fluent in English with a delightful sense of humour. Paul Brand, Ludwig and I (Paul later to become famous for his surgical discoveries among lepers) were particularly good friends and used to spend fascinating hours making fudge and reciting excerpts from *Winnie the Pooh.*

Most memorable of all were the evangelistic summer

treks when we would set out in two parties of a dozen men, equipped with a trek cart containing sleeping bags, a tent and a cooking pot, and five pounds to meet the requirements of the next two months. These treks covered over six hundred miles, in Ireland, Scotland, the Midlands and Wales, and provided us with opportunities for putting into practice some of the teaching of previous months.

The faith basis on which the Colony was run provided us with both a challenge and a blessing. It was a little startling, for instance, at our first prayer meeting in "Bethlehem"—the army hut set apart for Bible studies, lectures and devotional meetings—to hear Godfrey Buxton quietly announce that all grocery and other bills were paid up for the coming week, leaving a balance in the bank of seven shillings and sixpence. We used to joke about our monthly allowances, "ten bob per chap per month—perhaps!" But very rarely did the money fail, and if it did—or, as occasionally happened, the food began to run short—it drove us to our knees with a sense of urgency, not only for the present crisis but because if we couldn't learn now to prove the Lord as all sufficient, how could we expect to fare better overseas? I remember once experiencing a time of very real dearth, until God reminded us that there had been a grumbling spirit in the camp over the plethora of apples and pears from our orchard. Every meal had seen its quota of fruit served up in some form or other, and like the Israelites of old we began to yearn for the leeks and onions of Egypt. Only when this wrong attitude had been discovered and genuinely repented of did the money begin to flow in again, and all our needs were met once more.

Once, on trek in the Highlands of Scotland, our supplies ran out completely. There we were, twelve hungry young men having walked fifteen miles or more, with only a loaf of bread and half a pot of jam to sustain us. For the first and only time that trek we had to pitch our tent on the village green, as there wasn't even a church or chapel in the vicinity where we could be put up. Rarely was grace more fervently offered or a meal more quickly consumed. Afterwards we got down to prayer in real earnest—nor did those prayers go unheard. As we sallied forth from our tent to hold an open-air meeting, a Christian baker who lived in the village but worshipped some miles away, heard us singing and testifying and went home to his wife and asked her to get a meal ready for us. An hour later we were sitting down to a sumptuous feast. Then, as we prepared to return to our tent for the night, they asked if we could spare time the following morning to have breakfast with them. As we left the village the next day and went to the post office to collect any mail which might have arrived "post restante", we found—the only time on that trek—a letter which had been delayed, and in it a postal order for five pounds!

5

Every now and again some special speaker would be invited to lead us in a kind of spiritual retreat. Sometimes it would be an old Colony man, or somebody from the Japan Evangelistic Band, or W.E.C. I remember Norman Grubb praying at one such session, "Oh Lord, if we have to go through boiling oil, you will give us boiling oil grace!"

There were the half-nights of prayer which the more spiritual doubtless found a blessing, but for which many of us—myself included—were not nearly mature or spiritual enough. There was the temptation, without consciously being hypocritical, to utter fervent hallelujahs and amens, which I am afraid were often glib and superficial. I remember a brother snoring peacefully and audibly on his knees through many such devotional sessions, his snores equalled in volume only by his earnest ejaculations when awake. There is the story beloved by Colony men of one such meeting when earnest prayer was being offered, "Send us fire, Lord, send the fire!"—only to be interrupted by the Buxtons' housemaid bursting into the room and announcing, "The Crystal Palace is on fire!"

One day B.G. announced that we were to have a visit from a Dr. Joe Church, fresh from the revival in Ruanda. I remembered the young, recently-qualified Barts doctor who had given me a lift to the beach service at Paignton ten years earlier. When he actually arrived, I think we were all just a little disappointed. He cracked jokes, and his Biblical exegesis was distinctly suspect by some of the more orthodox among us. And yet there was an undefinable quality about this man, a transparency, a humility, which were singularly disarming.

I missed most of his talks (one could hardly call them lectures) as I was doing my "medical" at that time. This was a three month period which each of us spent in the casualty ward of the Croydon General Hospital; six weeks working as "junior" and six weeks as "senior" under the Casualty Officer. It was good experience and gave several a taste for medicine which eventually led them to further medical training—notably Paul Brand, to whom I have already referred. Most of us had previously taken an advanced Red Cross First Aid and A.R.P. course, but in addition to the normal bandaging and splinting required, we were now introduced to suturing, plastering and minor surgery. We assisted, moreover, in administering simple anaesthetics and attended post-mortems! Another practical part of our training included attendance at a dental clinic where in addition to sitting on the feet of recalcitrant patients under gas, we were instructed (though never, alas, allowed to practise) in the subtle art of tooth extraction.

In spite of missing most of Joe Church's talks, my fellow "medic" and I were both aware of the impact his visit was making on the rest of our brethren. Quite often a special speaker would arouse controversy on points of theological difference, but in this case there seemed only to be a growing conviction of sin—genuine repentance for wrong attitudes, jealousies, criticisms, which so quickly divide Christians from one another.

One evening Joe shared his testimony with us; how as an earnest young missionary eager to win souls to Christ, he had gone out to Ruanda with high ideals, expecting to find a jumping-off ground for Heaven, with super-saintly colleagues and instant converts ready to hand. Instead he found himself pitchforked into a famine situation. Malnutrition and disease were rife, and even worse, there was little of the fervent love and fellowship he had expected to find between missionary and missionary, let alone between missionary and African. Mass burials were being held with hundreds of corpses disposed of at a time in quicklime pits. Sick in body and mind, and even sicker at heart, Joe was persuaded to take a holiday in Kenya. Passing through Uganda he met again an African Christian, Simeon Nsibambi, to whom on a previous visit he had felt drawn. Nsibambi was well-educated, spoke quite good English and held a responsible position as a civil servant. He was also a substantial land owner. He and Joe had one great bond in common—a yearning after holiness; that hunger and thirst after righteousness which Jesus made a condition for blessing. As the two met again and shared something of their quest, and the disappointments they had encountered, they were drawn into a fellowship which transcended race, colour, language or culture. Joe postponed his visit to Kenya and for three days they met, intent on how they could come to possess experimentally the fullness of God's Holy Spirit. They used no commentaries but prayerfully searched the Scriptures, using Schofield references for every mention of Him in the Old and New Testaments. The Holy Spirit began to open their eyes to see, not only their own sinfulness, but God's remedy. "Why," asked Nsibambi, "has nobody ever told me before that I can be filled with the

Holy Spirit?" Joe wasn't quite sure how to answer. Nsibambi went on, "As far as I can see from what we have been reading in God's Word, He longs to fill any heart which is truly clean; we have read in 1 John 1 that 'The blood of Jesus Christ, God's Son, cleanses us from all sin', so what is to hinder us from claiming that cleansing and being filled now?" Together the two men claimed the cleansing of the blood of Christ, and by faith received the fullness of His Holy Spirit. Nothing startling appeared to happen, there were no immediate manifestations or signs, but both knew that their prayer had been answered.

Joe went on for his holiday in Kenya. Nsibambi resigned from his civil service job, gave much of his land to the Church and, although still a layman, began a preaching ministry of great effectiveness in a Church which had become cold and worldly. When Joe returned to Uganda from Kenya, he was asked by a rather irate missionary whatever he had been saying to Nsibambi to give him religious mania. As a medical man, Joe found Simeon completely sane, but with an overwhelming burden for those he now saw to be lost and perishing, without Christ and without hope in the world. Joe himself returned to Ruanda with a new awareness of sins forgiven, and with a new sensitivity to the Holy Spirit's prompting to ask forgiveness from those Africans he had grieved or hindered by hastiness, anger or irritability—sins which missionaries had been slow to acknowledge as such at all.

One of the first to be affected was Yosiya Kinuka, Joe's senior hospital assistant. He became not only a greatly beloved brother in Christ but also one of the outstanding leaders in the revival which gradually began to manifest itself throughout Ruanda, Burundi and Uganda, and ultimately the whole of East Africa.

This, then, was the substance of Joe Church's talk to us that evening. For many of us it seemed as if we had begun to catch a glimpse of the practical possible walk of holiness.

His vision for revival recognised no bounds. On his last evening with us at the Colony he shared something of his burden for Uganda, from where the founders of the Ruanda Mission had first set out. He spoke of its early pioneers, MacKay, Hannington, Pilkington and others and of the response to their message. We saw through his eyes the youthful pages in King Mwanga's court willing to be dismembered limb from limb and then thrown alive, singing, into the fire, rather than deny their new-found Saviour—martyrs whose blood indeed became the seed of the Church! He shared something of the heart-break of seeing a second generation of Christians growing up with little of the life and vitality of their predecessors, of a Church which to a tragic extent had become Christian only in name, in which under cover of nominal Christianity sins of witchcraft, adultery and drunkenness were nearly as rife as they had been in the old pagan days. He spoke, too, of the young Africans so recently set on fire in the revival from which he had just returned. So burning was their love for the Lord and for the precious souls for which He shed His blood, that they were nicknamed the "Abaka"—the fiery ones! We learned of Blasio Kigozi, a young ordained missionary to Ruanda, brother of Simeon Nsibambi, who only the previous year had died of fever contracted through spending nights in the tick-infested grass huts of those he sought to win for Christ. Also of his message to his own

Church of Uganda during its Jubilee Year 1936 to "Awake". He described the stirrings of the movement of the Holy Spirit in Uganda, as numbers responded to the good news they had almost forgotten, repenting and making costly restitution for sins committed, money stolen, broken homes; so much so that whereas in Ruanda the revived ones were known as the "Abaka", in Uganda the name given—largely in mockery—was "the saved ones" the "balokole"! We heard, too, of the young well educated Ugandan, William Nagenda, who with his wife Sala had offered to go to Ruanda as a missionary to take Blasio's place and of the way in which Blasio's mantle had fallen on him.

Finally, Joe Church told us of his vision of a team for Uganda—something like Hudson Taylor's Cambridge Seven which a generation before had gone out to evangelise China—seven young men who believed the Lord was calling them, not to Ruanda with all the thrill and excitement of revival, but to Uganda, to proclaim once again the good news of One who could save to the uttermost all who came to God by Him.

I was much moved by all I heard that evening, as were many of my fellow students; but of course it did not apply to me! Nancy and I were in close touch with E.U.S.A. on whose advice I had applied to the Colony—so what was the point of thinking about Africa? To my astonishment as we were leaving the Buxtons' house, Joe Church called me over and said, "I gather you would be willing to be one of the 'Uganda Seven'—can you come to see me tomorrow morning before I leave, and have a chat about it?" I was flabbergasted! It was the first I'd heard about it, and I wondered if by any chance he had remembered our previous encounter at Paignton. I heard later that the suggestion had come from Godfrey Buxton. Nor did our chat the following morning throw much light on the situation. If the Lord was calling me to Uganda, Joe was quite certain that somehow the way would open up. Meanwhile he suggested I contacted Dr. Wilson Cash, then General Secretary of C.M.S., who had expressed interest in the Uganda Seven project and had in principle given it his blessing.

Nancy and I were now officially engaged, so of course she was as much affected as myself by this startling new suggestion. The more we thought and prayed about it, however, the stronger became the conviction that we were meant to offer for Uganda. Our interest in the E.U.S.A. was still keen but we had always been attracted to the Mission rather than convinced that God wanted us in South America. First, though, we must be quite sure that this was God calling us to Uganda and not just a passing whim.

I wrote as Joe had suggested to C.M.S. and duly received an invitation to Headquarters, then situated in Salisbury Square, just off Fleet Street, for a chat with the Candidates' Secretary. That first interview was not an unqualified success. I was awkward and ill at ease, and he perhaps regarded me as a rather narrow and bigoted youngster with a bee in his bonnet regarding Africa. He did not seem to have heard anything about any Uganda Seven and obviously entertained doubts as to my suitability for it if there were such a scheme.

Later, I was again invited to Salisbury Square, this time to meet the Africa Secretary, Canon Hooper, for a more encouraging session. He spoke warmly of the Colony and of Godfrey Buxton with whom he had been at Cambridge; also of his good friend Joe Church! He assured me that my lack of academic qualifications, which I had begun to think might be affecting their decision, needn't necessarily prove a handicap to that particular work, and that the training I had already received should be quite acceptable to the Society. He, too, however doubted very much whether there was any suitable opening for me in Uganda. Would I be interested in evangelistic outreach in the Nuba Mountains? Or using my business experience in one of the C.M.S. bookshops? I replied that I believed God was calling me specifically to Uganda.

After several months of frustrating correspondence a particularly attractive suggestion was made. Would I care to work in Nairobi with the evangelist, Roland Pitway? Nancy and I were disturbed by this offer. *Had* God called us to work in Uganda, or were we being obstinate, following an imaginary will o' the wisp?

Once again I sought an interview with Canon Hooper, and shared with him our concern only to be in the place God meant us to be. He was understanding and sympathetic, this time disclosing the fact that the main reason the door to Uganda seemed closed was financial; there simply wasn't the money, especially in 1938 when C.M.S. was facing retrenchment rather than expansion, to send out even one more new recruit. In order for me to go to Uganda at least £1,000 would be required to cover my passage and support for four years. The affair immediately took on a much more hopeful aspect! If it was simply a question of finance...! Hadn't we proved again and again at the Colony that the Lord supplied all our needs? What was a £1,000 more or less to Him? Together we began to pray for the required sum. Two weeks later I was away taking part in a mission when a telegram arrived from the Colony: "£250 received for your support, Hallelujah". A quarter of the amount already. Soon after came news of an elderly widow who had heard of the Uganda Seven scheme and wanted to give a substantial sum in memory of her husband. It was exactly £1,000—could it be used for my support?

So, in less than a month, the whole amount had come in plus twenty-five per cent interest! The door to Uganda stood wide open.

6

"WHAT ABOUT CASTOR oil? A hot water bottle might give him some relief!" "Better call the doctor, his temperature is obviously rising!" Thus, somewhat unexpectedly, my career at the Colony came to its conclusion. I had been speaking at a women's meeting in the East End of London and as a treat was provided with crab salad. That night I woke feeling sick and in considerable pain. There was no alternative but to wake Peter Guillebaud who slept in the opposite bunk and ask his advice. Back came the above suggestions. All having been acted upon with varying degrees of success, I found myself ignominiously trundled—feet first—into an ambulance, bound for the familiar portals of Croydon General Hospital. The attack of food poisoning laid me low for three weeks in hospital where I lost nearly a stone in weight. My sailing to Africa with Bishop Stuart and the rest of the team was postponed for several months.

Once the required money had come in everything had gone like clockwork. Gifts in cash and kind were forthcoming for all my equipment; passport formalities, inoculations and all the paraphernalia of departure were completed—then this unexpected check. Satan, we were to discover, often expressed his disapproval in physical terms. Underlying the disappointment and perplexity, however, was a sense of peace and assurance. God had called me and in His own time I would get to Uganda.

On March 16th, 1939, I sailed from Tilbury on a dilapidated 8,000 ton vessel with a heavy starboard list, the S.S. *Durham Castle*, far removed from my childhood memories of the majestic *City of Poona*. A party had gathered on the platform at St. Pancras station to see off the boat train. Nancy was to follow me as quickly as home circumstances permitted, and we were to be married as soon as Mission regulations allowed. What an incentive to pass my language exams!

Mother meanwhile had sold our house at West Croydon and was living in comfortable rooms in Beulah Hill, near the Colony, where I had been able to pay her frequent visits. She had suffered a breakdown lasting nearly three months when I was first accepted for training, but had now made a complete recovery. She, too, was on the platform, serene and upheld for a parting which, though then we could never have imagined it, was to last seven and a half years. B.G. and others from Upper Norwood were there, too, and committed us—mother, Nancy and myself—to God in prayer. Once again we sang the familiar Colony chorus, which had never seemed more appropriate:

How good is the God we adore,
Our faithful, unchangeable friend,
Whose love is as great as His power
And knows neither measure nor end.

'Tis Jesus the first and the last
Whose Spirit shall guide us safe home,
We'll praise Him for all that is past
And trust Him for all that's to come.

The voyage, in spite of our rather cramped tourist

quarters, proved as enjoyable as it was leisurely, and afforded just the buffer that was required between the trauma of uprooting from one way of life and adapting to another. I feel sorry for missionary recruits these days, and those returning to the field, who can no longer enjoy the gradual transition such a journey afforded; who instead find themselves jetted in a matter of hours from one environment to another. We stopped at almost every port, getting severely sunburned at Port Sudan, swindled at Port Said and surfeited at Port Suez!

We had quite a missionary party on board and enjoyed prayer, Bible Study and fellowship. One of our number was returning to Mboga (now Boga-Zaire) to resume the work begun among the pygmies by the saintly Apolo Kivibulaya. He enthralled us with colourful stories of his first term of service in Africa. Another member of our party proved as good a teacher as she was Luganda scholar. I owe her much for she laid the foundations during those four weeks of a grasp of Luganda which enabled me, by the time we reached our destination, at least to exchange greetings and understand a few phrases. This was a great encouragement as I had dreaded learning a language so unlike anything I had known before.

Early one morning, four weeks after leaving Tilbury docks, we sailed into Mombasa harbour to set foot for the first time on East African soil. We spent a chaotic day in the moist heat of that historic coastal town retrieving our luggage, passing through customs and exploring some of the narrow streets which not so long before had echoed to the harsh sounds and sights of the slave trade. The following afternoon we boarded the train for the forty-eight-hour journey up 9,000 feet, through the highlands of Kenya, and down again to

Kampala, capital of Uganda. I couldn't help comparing our journey, hot, dusty and rather cramped as it was, with that of our predecessors making their painful way on foot in a safari lasting three months or more. One thought of the dangers they braved from disease, wild animals and hostile tribes; also of the many, James Hannington for one, who had laid down their lives to open the door for the Gospel in East Africa. There were the fascinating glimpses from the train of game—buck, giraffe, zebra and ostrich—and the welcome break at Nairobi where we spent a few hours with missionaries; the first astonishing sight of the Rift Valley; bargaining at wayside stations with eager, smiling vendors of pineapple, mango, passion fruit, bananas and other tropical fruit at incredibly low prices. Finally, the thrill of waking the second morning to hear at last Luganda as it was really spoken, and the halting attempts to use the greetings laboriously learned on board ship, and the even greater thrill of finding them understood!

We travelled on through seemingly endless tracts of banana plantations interspersed with sugar cane, coffee and tea, until about midday we crossed the bridge over the Ripon Falls and saw the source of the Nile, discovered only sixty years earlier. Three hours later we arrived at Kampala. Here a splendid welcome awaited us as we were whisked off to various Mission bungalows on Namirembe, "the hill of Peace", crowned with its handsome red brick Cathedral. I found myself staying with Bishop Stuart, the kindest and most hospitable of hosts.

That same evening I had my first encounter with the "balokole" of whom I had heard so much. Their faces seemed alight, and after the usual exchange of greetings with which I was becoming familiar, they dived straight in with their testimony of how Jesus had met and saved them. After a pause came a question which, even from them, took me aback: "Are you saved?" What a thing to ask! Wasn't I a missionary, trained at the Colony what's more! Surely I was there to teach *them*—not to be asked such personal questions. However, I knew what they meant and was glad to reply in the affirmative. "Praise the Lord!" was their response. "Tell us all about it!" I was quite prepared to give my testimony in detail, and told how my parents had been missionaries in India and brought me up to know and love the Lord Jesus; how at the age of six I had accepted Him as my personal Saviour. They again expressed their happiness; then came a further pause, followed by yet another question. "And what's happening *now*?" It really was too bad, asking a stranger such searching and personal questions—who did they think they were anyhow? But deep down, in spite of my resentment, the seeds of conviction had been sown. I was unable to answer their third question because although I undoubtedly knew Jesus Christ as my Saviour from the guilt and penalty of sin, I had yet to discover my need of Him to save me from its power and dominion. I had no up-to-date testimony of what was happening now.

"Beware," said a wise man, "of the barrenness of a busy life." "Yes," came the reply, "but beware, too, of the busy-ness of a barren life!" Those first months in Uganda were certainly busy, but equally barren of anything spiritual. There were the usual problems of acclimatisation, best described as heat, humidity and height (4,000 feet above sea level is a factor to be reckoned with). Then there was the culture shock of a totally different way of life—different food, different habits and patterns of behaviour, and a completely unfamiliar language structure. Added to all this there was an aching sense of separation from loved ones, although mail was regular and frequent (all letter mail at that time was automatically by air, taking just four days and costing a penny halfpenny for two ounces). However, no number of letters could compensate for the fact that both Nancy and my mother, with other relatives and friends, were over 4,000 miles away, a full month's journey. On the surface I appeared cheerful and content, making good progress with language study and writing glowing descriptions of my new surroundings, but there was something lacking for which no amount of activity could compensate.

Two days after my arrival in Uganda Bishop Stuart licensed me as a Diocesan layreader, located to Bulemezi, a district thirty miles east of Kampala. The Bishop himself, who couldn't have been kinder to a raw recruit, ran me out by car to Ndejje, where I was to concentrate mainly on language study—conducting at weekends a programme of refresher courses for clergy and evangelists. In this I was to be assisted by an attractive young deacon, Galiwango, one of the balokole, acting as my interpreter. In addition to a large church, day schools and maternity centre, Ndejje boasted a flourishing girls' boarding school run by a missionary Pattie Drakely, who with her elderly mother out on a protracted visit, made me feel at home. I had my meals with them while living by myself in a nearby annexe, a most satisfactory arrangement.

The Africans seemed happy to have me in Bulemezi, bestowing on me the African name Ssebowa—son of Bowa—a nearby hill. Yet not far beneath the surface there lurked strains and tensions. Not long after arriving at Ndejje, I discovered through Galiwango that a pastor in a neighbouring village was living with four women, baptising his illegitimate children at home in order to make them Christians. When, deeply shocked, I reported the matter to the authorities I was assured that he would be retiring in two years' time, when it was hoped to replace him with a better man! There were similar shocks, making it all too evident that the general level of Christianity was at an appallingly low ebb. There seemed little difference between Christians, so called, and their pagan neighbours. Drunkenness, immorality and witchcraft abounded, but the church appeared to have little concern, let alone an answer.

Galiwango and his wife, and one of the teachers in the school were certainly different. They exhibited a quality of life which singled them out. But even they were difficult to understand. Their standards were so high and there were times when they seemed actually to doubt where I stood spiritually.

After a couple of months at Ndejje, I was supposed to move to Luwero, another church centre in Bulemezi, this time with no missionary near at hand. This raised the important question of transport. On our weekly shopping expeditions to Kampala I had for some time been on the look out for a second-hand motorcycle for about twenty pounds—all I had managed to save in the time. Just ten days before moving I looked in again at an Asian-owned garage to enquire if they had anything suitable, and discovered that although they had no motorbike I could have an ancient 1928 Hillman car for seventeen pounds ten shillings. It seemed in good condition, sporting a canvas hood and a capacious "dickey" at the back—the gear lever moved in a kind of open cage, which for one who had never previously driven a car was a distinct advantage. I drove back to Ndejje that morning, the proud possessor of a car which lasted several years and many thousands of miles over dusty corrugated Uganda roads. The following week I drove it in again to Kampala to pass my driving test—a much less stringent affair than today—and then straight on to my new headquarters at Luwero.

I was accompanied by Bugs, a recently acquired puppy, and George, a diminutive but lively monkey; also by Erifazi, my general factotum who, for twenty-five shillings a month cooked, valeted, laundered and generally cared for my well-being. Our arrival at Luwero was quite an occasion, with the school band—three instruments and some African drums headed by a Union Jack—turning out in our honour! By nightfall we were installed in a little three-roomed African hut, complete with mud walls, thatched roof and dung-smeared floor, furnished with the camp equipment I had taken out with me.

Three nights later I was roused by an urgent hammering on the door. A distraught voice begged me to get the car out. The wife of the voice's owner was about to have a baby and the nearest maternity centre was Ndejje, thirty miles away. I had never previously driven at night and indeed had driven less than one hundred miles altogether. However we got the car started up. After less than five miles there was renewed excitement in the dickey. The babe had arrived! Recollecting what I could of Colony first aid, though we had never advanced as far as midwifery, I shouted over my shoulder such appropriate encouragement and instructions as I could, meanwhile stepping manfully on the accelerator. An hour later I assisted a remarkably calm young mother and her baby out of the car, accompanied by a distinctly shaken father.

Later they asked me to become godfather to their little daughter, the first of many such invitations.

The months spent at Luwero passed quickly. My Luganda improved, and I preached my first faltering sermon in less than four months, taking the first language exam in six. Galiwango and I still teamed up each week-end, visiting one church centre or another for retreats and refresher courses, similar to that first held at Ndejje. Meanwhile the clouds of war loomed threateningly on the horizon. News from home became steadily worse, until in September 1939 war was declared.

Every available single man was called up. I had already been to Kampala for a preliminary medical overhaul and expected my call-up papers at any moment. The Bishop, however, was nothing if not a statesman and realised that unless he acted promptly he would be left with virtually no male missionaries at all. Despite the Scriptural injunction to lay hands suddenly on no man, he decided to kill two birds with one stone—to ordain me, and fill an essential gap at the Bishop Tucker Theological College at Mukono. So, on St. Andrew's day, November 30th, 1940, I found myself ordained deacon in St. Paul's Cathedral, Namirembe, with a new and completely unexpected job ahead of me as tutor at Mukono, where our African pastors and evangelists received their training.

So began a period which proved to be the bleakest and most barren of my life. Mystics have written of the "dark night of the soul" and while laying no personal claim to mysticism, I discovered during these months something of what they meant.

Apart from anything else this was my first introduction to liberal theology, in fairly massive doses at that! My previous reading had been confined to the Scriptures, in which we had received a thorough grounding at the Colony, and a few standard evangelical textbooks. I was confused and bewildered by much of what I was supposed to be teaching. Moreover every lecture I gave had to be translated into Luganda, so that I was burning a good deal of midnight oil. Because we were so short-staffed I soon found myself, in addition to a full teaching programme, acting as College Bursar and to some extent responsible for building and maintenance. Life was undoubtedly busy, and undoubtedly barren. An inferiority complex, of which I had been unaware, began to assume vast proportions. My missionary colleagues, though friendly, belonged to a different school of thought from that in which I had been brought up. At the same time my attitude to Africans, staff and students alike, bore a distinctly colonial flavour, admitting little in the way of real friendship. Nor were things too happy in the College itself. Many of the students in training had no assurance or even clear understanding of salvation. Most of them reflected the attitude widely prevailing in the Church of Uganda at that time, that provided they were baptised and confirmed and *not discovered* in any particular wrongdoing, they were Christians. Stealing in the College was rife as, to some extent, were drinking and immorality. Against this gloomy background a dozen or so students stood out sharply. Their faces shone. Their testimony, sometimes misunderstood, often resented, challenged all who heard it, as did their manner of life.

I found myself peculiarly affected by all this. I was familiar with so much for which they stood, though still remaining on the sidelines—a singularly uncomfortable position—and one which had to be resolved. But how?

7

"DEAR BILL," WROTE Joe Church, "could you join me in a Mission to Fort Portal on your next vacation? It would be grand to link up with you again!" I felt rather flattered to be invited to join in such an effort. There was bound to be blessing; moreover the "balokole" would then have to accept me, and not regard me with such suspicion. Hardly the worthiest motives for accepting such an invitation, though understandable perhaps, considering how unhappy I was at the time. But then came a further letter saying how delighted Joe was that I could go; would I please take with me in my car Simeoni Nsibambi, William Nagenda and Benoni Kagwa, my co-Chaplain on the staff at Mukono, and one of the balokole. A journey of over two hundred miles involving a whole day with men I could hardly tolerate, who disapproved of me and had certainly (and this was very humiliating) been praying for me! It was too much, and yet I had written to say I would go, and my pride would scarcely permit me to withdraw. Desperately I prayed that God might smite me with malaria or dysentery. Anything that would enable me, without loss of face, to avoid that journey. It was at just that point three days before we were due to set out, when I was so unhappy, sleeping badly and on the verge, it may well have been, of a breakdown, that God had sent Yokana with his urgent plea to "go and see the lady missionary from Ruanda!" as told in the first chapter. The whole picture miraculously changed! William, whom I had detested and feared, became overnight a beloved brother. The mote I had seen so clearly in his eye, I now saw as a great beam in my own, and the journey I had feared so much became one of many when "Jesus Himself drew near and went with us".

We broke our journey at Namutamba, where we spent the weekend. I had heard of Leslie Lea-Wilson, a Christian tea-planter and cattle owner, who ran a big tea estate fifty-four miles from Kampala, which he supplied with milk from his own farm. This was my first meeting with one who was to be a lifelong friend. As well as being a staunch evangelical, Leslie was a shrewd businessman. He had spent years in Uganda and knew many Africans who, professing to be Christians, cheerfully stole, lied and committed adultery like any pagan. A year or two previously, however, a team of revived brethren led by William had visited Namutamba, as a result of which many of the workers on the estate were converted. To Leslie's astonishment they came to him confessing and making costly restitution for thefts and other sins they had committed. As a practical outcome the following week the milk yield was almost doubled! One of the herdsmen was converted and at once realised he could no longer continue stealing milk as he and his companions had regularly been doing. Tremendous pressure was put on him by his friends as they realised that if he returned full milk pails, theirs would appear half empty! He was beaten up on several occasions, his hut was burned down and attempts were even made to poison him but all to no avail. In the end he emerged triumphant, for through his fearless testimony many of his fellow herdsmen came to know Jesus Christ. Not long after he, with a number of others, was prepared for baptism and took the appropriate name, Peter. Due in no small measure to his witness, Namutamba became a centre of new life, exerting a greater influence for good than many mission stations.

From Namutamba we drove on to Fort Portal, my first visit to the Western Province of Uganda, where we found Joe and others of the team already gathered. For the first time in two years I found myself part of a warm loving fellowship in which Jesus was manifestly active. The preaching was powerful, plentifully illustrated from personal testimony, and many came to know Jesus Christ for the first time as Saviour and Lord. It was thrilling to catch at first hand a glimpse of what God was beginning to do all over East Africa.

After that mountain-top experience came the journey back to the valley, where the vision so clearly given had to be worked out in the day to day routine of a theological college. First I had to go to the Bishop and ask his forgiveness for so much personal failure and compromise. This was by no means easy, for he had been exceedingly kind to me and I knew he was very anxious lest the balokole movement, with many of whose aims he was essentially in sympathy, might split the Church of Uganda. His advisers, almost to a man, condemned the movement as dangerous and divisive, and now I had to go and tell him that I believed God was leading me into total identification with it. Nor indeed was it easy for him to accept. Even more difficult was my interview with the Warden of Mukono, a brilliant scholar who had himself been blessed through the aftermath of the Welsh revival but had strangely little sympathy with what he regarded as a subversive movement, threatening all he held most dear within the church. To describe the situation at Mukono as delicate would be a laughable understatement. Mistakes were undoubtedly made, bricks dropped, and toes trodden on as tension built up.

And yet throughout that period, lasting several months, God was at work in the College. A handful of balokole were meeting at four o'clock every morning to pray for revival, and numbers increased almost daily. I had held serious doubts as to the advisability of such early rising. Right at the commencement of the new term I met with the brethren to share with them my new found testimony and re-discovered joy in the Lord, receiving from them the same overwhelming love and welcome that William and others at Fort Portal had already extended to me. I shared with them, too, my misgiving as to whether I could possibly rise at such an early hour—feeling sure that they would understand my point of view. It soon became apparent, however, they didn't understand at all! The Lord had looked after them physically for nearly two years, and blessed them in their early morning fellowship; couldn't He do the same for me? Gently, without exerting any pressure, they asked if I wouldn't try it for a week and see what happened. If after that I felt it was too much for me they would quite understand, but why not give God a chance? With considerable misgivings I set my alarm next day for four o'clock, and very soon that early morning tryst became a time I couldn't miss. Often the whole two hours would be spent in praise, adoration and worship. On occasions a passage from the Bible would spark into life as though God was literally speaking to us. Yet again there were times when things needed to be put right between brother and brother, sins confessed and forgiven—sometimes with tears—before the breakthrough could take place, and God manifest His power in our midst. Meanwhile an already overfull programme was maintained from rising bell at six a.m. to nine or ten at night. Such early rising would not always be necessary or wise, but those were exceptional times, calling for exceptional measures. This went on for three months, until early one morning I was suddenly seized with violent pains and had to be rushed into Mengo Hospital, where a few hours later I was relieved of a seriously inflamed appendix.

None of us was altogether surprised to find on my return from three weeks convalescence in Kenya that I had been posted elsewhere! First to Masindi, in Bunyoro, for six weeks and then to Nyakasura School, Fort Portal, over two hundred miles away in the Western Province of Uganda! I was obviously an embarrassment to my colleagues on the staff who, with the exception of the Rev. Benoni Kagwa, were united in their determination to stamp out what they regarded as a potentially dangerous group within the College, and I can appreciate their dilemma. I shall never forget our farewell meeting, or the hymn we sang as I drove away from Mukono at six o'clock one morning:

> Oh that will be glory, glory, glory,
> O that will be glory
> When we meet to part no more.

Ten days later I heard from a party of A.I.M. missionaries passing through near-by Masindi, that twenty-five students had been expelled from Mukono as rebels.

Getting straight into the car I drove through the night to Kampala, and made my way to Nsibambi's house, as I felt sure he would be able to tell me just what had happened. There sure enough I found some of the "rebels" full of peace and joy, camping out in his compound. Only a few days after my departure three notices had gone up on the board:

1. No student was to leave his dormitory before the rising bell at six a.m.
2. No student was allowed to preach within the College precincts without permission from the Warden.
3. Students were forbidden to meet together in groups exceeding three in number.

There could be no doubt as to whom the new rules applied, and they posed an agonising choice. These were not angry young men or callow youths, accustomed to flouting authority. Most of them were married men with families—mature Christians who had already spent several years actively engaged in full-time Christian service; many were within only a few months of ordination. They pleaded with the College authorities to rescind the rules, but to no avail. They spent the half-term holiday in prayer and fasting, before reaching the costly conclusion that in this particular situation they had no alternative but to obey God rather than man. The following morning they rose as usual for prayer and fellowship at four a.m. Their names were taken as they came from the meeting and submitted to the Warden. One by one they were solemnly expelled from the College, their licence to preach in the Church of Uganda withdrawn, and they were branded as rebels. The Bishop was away on safari at the time, or such severe measures might never have been taken.

My outstanding memory of those days was the spirit in which my African brethren accepted what could so easily have led to anger, resentment or frustration. Far from feeling ill-treated, they could only praise that they were counted worthy to suffer a little for the sake of their Master. Had Satan won a resounding victory? Nothing could be further from the truth! For a time the Church of Uganda had lost some of its potential leadership, but this was God's means of scattering them throughout Uganda. For nearly seven years the revival, so long awaited and so earnestly prayed for, seemed to lie dormant. Yet, almost unrealised, the seed sown often in tears, was to reap a harvest.

8

"ARE YOU TWO really one?" The question came as something of a bombshell to Bob Freak and myself. For three months we had been trying to make the best of a bad job! Neither of us would have chosen the other as a colleague. We were so completely different, temperamentally and in every way—yet here we were, desperately under-staffed and over-worked, dumped together in a boys' secondary boarding school over two hundred miles from the capital.

Nyakasura was a unique establishment. Founded by a naval commander with highly original ideas, it had flourished during the pre-war years. Its unusual uniform of khaki kilts and red stockings was known and admired throughout the Western Province, and "the Commander" had left his mark in countless other ways. Chapel services, to give an example, were enlivened by the organ he had built himself which in turn was powered from a small hydro-electric turbine he had built and installed.

In 1941 with four European staff called up, we were hard put to it to maintain his high standards. Although Bob was eminently well-qualified as a teacher, I had never previously taught except for the time at Mukono when teaching had been almost entirely in the vernacular. Shortage of food, petrol and clothing made our task no easier, and although our surroundings were idyllic we had little leisure to enjoy them. Less than five miles away rose the foothills of the snowcapped Ruwenzori Range —the "Mountains of the Moon". The country around was lush and green and beautiful, with its hills, valleys and crater lakes, although some of the latter held the dubious reputation, apart from being "bottomless", of being infested with evil spirits.

Lovely as were our surroundings, little mannerisms and habits tended to irritate, and trifling differences magnified out of all proportion. Bob, like myself, had been challenged by the mission in Fort Portal a few months earlier but neither of us had, as yet, discovered how to work it out in the realm of personal relationships; and though we prayed together every day we found increasing difficulty in doing so. Some of our African brethren, somehow sensing that things weren't going too well, cycled the two hundred and sixteen dusty miles from Kampala to have fellowship and encourage us. This, of course, was one of the hidden assets accruing from the seeming tragedy of the Mukono expulsions, and one which the devil must surely have overlooked! Teams were now free as never before to travel throughout the country strengthening and encouraging one another, and building others up in the Lord. The fact that they were prepared to do so, travelling hundreds of miles, gives some indication of their love and concern.

In due course they arrived at Nyakasura, hot, dusty and tired, but overflowing with the love and joy of the Lord. That evening sitting with us round a wood fire (it could be quite cold at 6,000 feet after the sun had set) they spoke naturally and freely of the Lord, sharing up-to-date testimonies of His gracious dealings with them. One thing led to another until, out of the blue, came that unexpected question, "Are you two really one?" We weren't of course and we knew it. But somehow in that relaxed atmosphere we could afford to be honest with each other, and the Lord enabled us little by little to bring out into His searching light the hidden things which had built up into formidable barriers. "If we walk in the light, as He is in the light", we read in 1 John 1, verse 7, "we have fellowship with one another and the blood of Jesus Christ, God's Son, cleanses us from all sin". It seemed so simple—the greatest truths so often are! Although neither of us found it easy—indeed it was very costly to open our hearts to one another in such a way—the foundations were laid that evening of a deep and enduring fellowship which lasted the whole four years we were together at Nyakasura and long after. There were still occasional petty rubs and irritations, and the clash of strong personalities, but now we knew what to do about them, they were robbed of their previous power to frustrate and separate us. The school, too, was quick to sense the change in our relationship and was no longer able to play us off against each other.

Meanwhile, at home in England Nancy was facing problems of a different sort. Her father's death soon after I sailed for Uganda made it possible for her to offer to C.M.S. for training as a missionary fiancée. 1940 saw her installed at Foxbury, in Chislehurst, Kent until the growing menace of nightly air-raids rendered it advisable to move. This was to Ridley Hall, Cambridge, thanks to an unusually heavy air-raid which coincided with a lecturing visit to Foxbury by the Principal of Ridley. Moved to compassion at the sight of female recruits leaping about on the roof in their night attire, extinguishing incendiary bombs (in which rescue operations he himself, lightly clad in striped pyjamas and a mackintosh took an active part), the Rev. Paul Gibson decided it was time for Cambridge to come to the rescue. The number of theological students at Ridley having been drastically depleted by the call-up, an entire wing was available, and placed at the disposal of those in training at Foxbury. Within a few days the cloistered calm of Ridley was shattered, and such men as were fortunate enough to be in residence, entered on a new and quite unique phase of pastoral preparation.

Those were good months for Nancy. Cambridge life suited her and she even began to put on some weight. While not entirely in agreement with all she was taught there, she had a sincere affection and respect for Florence Allshorn—a remarkable pioneer in missionary training methods. Florence paid Nancy the compliment of describing her as "a rough diamond, but a diamond none the less!" Even after she had completed her training, however, the future remained uncertain. Boats to Africa were few, and Nancy was eventually advised to return to her work as a dispenser until a passage became available. She had little difficulty in obtaining a suitable post, but as month followed month and nothing further was heard of a sailing date, she couldn't help wondering at times when, if ever, we would be reunited.

At last, eighteen months after she had first packed, came the summons. Late one Friday evening, arriving home through the now familiar blackout, a mysterious voice enquired over the phone whether Nancy could be ready to sail the following Tuesday. A hectic scramble followed. All her books, long since crated and awaiting despatch, had to be unpacked, censored and re-crated again; and the numerous wedding presents, china and household goods which had accumulated during the years we were engaged made ready for despatch. Security was so strict she didn't know until the night before she sailed which port to make for.

The voyage itself—much of which was in convoy through submarine infested waters—was hardly luxurious. A strictly enforced blackout required all portholes to be tightly sealed and there were frequent alarms and excursions. Two ships in the convoy were torpedoed. There was general rejoicing when, at last, after nearly seven weeks, the ship arrived at Capetown amid an unfamiliar blaze of lights.

The final stage of the journey—three days by rail over the "garden route" to Durban where, miraculously, Nancy secured a passage to Mombasa—passed comparatively smoothly. The voyage, in a small coasting vessel, was enlivened by innumerable cockroaches and other insects. Nancy was intrigued, too, by the deck passengers travelling with their goats and cattle, which often succeeded in breaking loose and running along the passenger decks! Eventually, she was able to send off the long awaited cable telling me the date she expected to arrive at Mombasa, and subsequently by train to Kampala. For some reason her cable was delayed and I received it only the day before she was due to arrive! There was barely time to travel the two hundred and sixteen miles to Namirembe where I spent a somewhat sleepless night before driving in a borrowed car to meet her at Jinja, fifty miles down the line. Little did either of us then imagine how well we would come to know that little town at the source of the Nile, where eventually we spent thirteen years of our married life.

After a separation of three and a half years we were

reunited. Our joy at being together again was, however, tinged with a bitter disappointment. The original plan, endorsed by C.M.S. Headquarters at home, had been that we should be married shortly after Nancy's arrival in Uganda. To her astonishment and dismay, she found a letter awaiting her at Mombasa briefly informing her that, owing to war-time regulations, she must serve at least one year's unmarried service! She was to proceed therefore as quickly as possible to Hoima, a place she had never heard of, one hundred and forty miles across country from Nyakasura, there to join the staff of the Girls' Secondary Boarding School. Neither of us found this delay easy to understand or to accept. It seemed unfair and unnecessary and we couldn't help feeling that it reflected the disapproval of those in authority for our balokole sympathies. We had yet to learn that whatever man may do, God makes no mistake!

In the welcoming throng at Hoima which surrounded her Nancy noticed some whose faces really seemed to shine. On enquiring who they were she was told that they were balokole!

Her three European colleagues had all been blessed in those early days of revival. Miss Wright, her senior missionary, "Amoti" the uncrowned Queen of Bunyoro, as she was sometimes known, was a saintly woman, due to leave shortly for South Africa on retirement, and Nancy's first task was to help her pack up her belongings. The other two, Lucy and Margaret, with whom later Nancy shared a mission bungalow, were very different from each other but had both been learning the same lessons which God was teaching Bob and me at Nyakasura. They welcomed Nancy warmly and helped her in every possible way, but they too were overdue for leave in South Africa, as home leave during the war years was out of the question. Soon Nancy was left, the only European woman on the mission station, a raw recruit with no teaching experience whatever, to help run a large girls' boarding school. Had it not been for the African brethren, life would indeed have been difficult. Knowing little of the country and even less of the language, with 140 miles separating us, she could have felt desperately lonely and miserable; in fact that year proved an outstandingly happy one for her!

It started at the daily fellowship meeting when, in the cool of the evening, a handful of balokole met together in the "kaju", a little hut set aside for prayer and fellowship. After one of these meetings an African brother took her gently aside and said in his rather broken English, "We love the thoughts and verses you bring to us from God's Word and they are very good and helpful, but we don't really know you any better now than when you first came to Hoima." Nancy's immediate reaction was "And why should you?" She painstakingly explained to him that as a Scot she had been brought up to believe that reserve was a good thing and that to wear one's heart on one's sleeve was the essence of bad form. Swizin didn't seem impressed by her argument, going so far as to enquire whether she had ever thought that her reserve, of which she was so proud, might be sin. That set Nancy thinking. She was honest and had to admit that there was an openness and infectious joy among these balokole which she found most attractive. Had she, as a sister in Christ, any right to erect a barrier of reserve from her African brothers and sisters; or did pride or fear hold her back?

Nancy began to discover for herself, as I had, the joy of a warm loving fellowship in which she could blossom and unfold and be herself with no mask and no pretence. Florence Nganjali, a senior member of the African staff, became her greatest friend and mentor and later, when Nancy fell ill with a heavy dose of malaria, it was Florence who looked after her and nursed her with tenderness and care. In fact, when her year of unmarried service was at last completed, and the day to which we had looked forward so long and so eagerly was actually within sight, Nancy almost wept. Not, let me hasten to add, because she no longer wanted to marry me, but because it meant leaving Hoima where she had learnt so much and made such lasting friendships.

Our wedding day dawned on October 22nd, 1943, twelve years after we first met. More than four hundred brethren joined us from all over Uganda and Ruanda, some travelling hundreds of miles. We held two receptions; one lasting nearly three days became a sort of mini-convention at a near-by church; the other was for fifty invited guests, African and European, at the Mountains of the Moon Hotel. In fact we had two of everything! Two best men, William Nagenda and Bob Freak; two clergymen to marry us, Erica Sabiti, later Archbishop of Uganda, and Cecil Markby, Principal of the Teacher Training College adjoining Nyakasura School, who with his wife Patience offered us boundless kindness and hospitality. The Markby children, together with their cousin Christopher Billington, provided Nancy with charming little attendants. Although, of course, we missed the presence of any relatives, we were surrounded and upheld by so many of our newfound family that we could not feel lonely or cut off, while

Leslie Lea-Wilson substituted as "Dad" to give Nancy away. We could only afford the three days of half-term for our honeymoon, as Bob was also overdue for leave and left us on our own soon after the wedding.

It was wonderful to be together at last in our little bungalow under the shadow of the Ruwenzori mountains. We were exceedingly happy, though with very little leisure to enjoy our new home. Nancy threw herself with characteristic energy into the work of the school, teaching English, running a dispensary, mothering the juniors and keeping open house. Later on we enjoyed a six-week holiday at Mombasa, in lieu of extended leave in South Africa, which left us high on the list for home leave when that eventually became possible.

During our time in Mombasa we met a number of Christian servicemen to whom we gave an open invitation to spend their leave with us at the Mountains of the Moon. Many made a thousand mile journey in order to do so, as a result of which we gained some wonderful friends.

Earlier, we lost our first child through a miscarriage. We were situated five miles from the Government dispensary and nearest doctor, and by the time he reached us it was all over. In January 1946, however, we had the joy of welcoming our first-born, Anne Elizabeth, into our hearts and homes. How thrilled we were. But not more so than our African brethren and the schoolboys who were almost as delighted as we were to welcome an English baby to Nyakasura. Unknown to us, however, problems lay ahead.

9

"WILL MR. BUTLER please report at once to the doctor's surgery!" Twice the message boomed out over the loudspeakers of the M.V. *Winchester Castle*. A large party of missionaries were travelling home together in 1946, soon after World War II ended, having done an unusually long term in Africa of nearly eight years. In those days, of course, we invariably journeyed by boat, air travel still being in its expensive infancy.

Nancy had had a very difficult time since giving birth to Anne and had subsequently spent several weeks in Mengo Hospital. Even when we returned to Fort Portal high temperatures persisted, sometimes soaring to 104°, leaving her weak and listless. It became increasingly evident that she would have to return to England as quickly as possible. We were delighted, therefore, to find ourselves homeward bound in company with Joe and Decie Church and several other friends whose leave was also overdue. Conditions were distinctly spartan. Single state rooms held as many as six female occupants, while we men slept in vast dormitories of three hundred or more three-tiered "stretchers" cunningly fitted into what used to be the gymnasium, swimming pool and even baggage holds, but at least we were able to relax from the strains and tensions of past months. Within a day or two we had organised a regular children's service attended by virtually every child on board, and in the evenings quite a large party of us would meet under the stars on the boat deck for Bible Study. Nancy seemed to be picking up too, her appetite was better and Anne, lulled by the regular beat of the ship's engines, was adapting splendidly to the routine of life on board ship, sleeping and eating well, with many willing nannies to share in looking after her.

Soon after leaving Aden Nancy went down again with a high temperature. Previously she had been given quinine on the assumption that she was suffering from chronic malaria, but this time even that seemed to have no effect. Things went rapidly from bad to worse. Anne, now five months old, had to be abruptly weaned and Nancy was taken into the ship's hospital where several missionary nurses devotedly "specialed" her. Then, just as we were entering the Suez Canal, came the dramatic summons. I had been spending as much time as I could with Nancy, but had just gone up on deck to cool off. It had been very hot in the Red Sea and was hotter still in the Canal. Even in the air-conditioned ship's hospital my shirt was wringing with perspiration within a minute or two. On reporting to the surgery, I found that Nancy's temperature had now risen to 106·2°, which, in spite of ice packs and everything that could be done for her, refused to come down. The ship's doctor, overworked with such a large complement of passengers on board, was exceedingly worried and only too grateful for Joe's offer of a consultation. Together they decided she must be suffering from some sort of sepsis and rigged up an intravenous penicillin drip. The doctor was very frank: Nancy, he told me, was dying. The only glimmer of hope he could offer was if she could survive the Canal and be admitted to the British hospital at Port Said, used specifically for merchant seamen, or emergency cases such as this. Instructions were radioed by ship's wireless, so that when we reached Port Said in the early hours of the following morning, we found a launch and an ambulance waiting. In less than an hour of landing, Nancy, still desperately ill, was in a hospital bed.

Riots were taking place in Port Said at the time, so that no vessels were able to dock in the normal way, nor were our friends allowed to accompany us off the ship.

I shall never forget seeing Nancy, unconscious, strapped to a stretcher, being lowered into the waiting launch. Nor the sight of Anne's pram (with Anne inside, fortunately sound asleep!) bumping down the companionway. Nor of hearing one of the sailors call out, "Careful with that pram, mate, there's a baby in it!" Nor am I likely ever to forget the awful sense of desolation the following day when passing the docks I saw that the *Winchester Castle* had already sailed, and with her all our friends. It was a rock bottom experience through which the Lord allowed us to pass, and yet in it all, in spite of our fears and faithlessness and sometimes despair, He proved Himself altogether faithful.

There was the meeting with Ek Mek Yan, for instance. As I was wandering somewhat disconsolately through the bazaar, the day after our arrival in Port Said, my eye caught sight of a kiosk bearing the familiar letters B. and F.B.S. It was an unpretentious little stall, manned by an unpretentious little man, whom I discovered to be an Armenian refugee. To my joy he proved to be a Christian bearing a bright witness in that unsalubrious neighbourhood. When I asked him where he worshipped he told me of a Gospel Hall run by some interdenominational American missionaries, which was also a meeting place for Christian troops. He told me it was quite some distance away, in fact just next door to the British hospital! The friends at the Peniel Mission could not have been kinder and did all that they could to help us.

Then there was the Russian doctor at the hospital itself, a brilliant diagnostician, who treated Nancy with the utmost care and consideration. Staunchly professing to be an atheist, he became God's messenger to us and a good friend. It was he who discovered the massive abscess which had been causing Nancy's acute septicaemia, and who secured the services of a Greek surgeon and an Egyptian anaesthetist to operate on her. Later he called in a French paediatrician to attend Anne who was next on the danger list with enteritis, and whom we nearly lost. She became an emaciated little bag of skin and bones and it took several months to nurse her back to health. The Egyptian nurses, many of them trained in mission hospitals, helped to make Nancy's stay endurable, although nothing could make her enjoy the diet of rice pudding made with buffalo milk and garlic-flavoured hard-boiled eggs.

We came to know some interesting folk in hospital, including a little Maltese lady whose daughter used to visit her regularly. When we asked if she had any other children she calmly announced that she had twenty-four with never a twin to lighten the load!

When the time came for us to leave the British hospital, Dr. Saunders, our Russian friend, refused to charge any fee for over a month's attendance and treatment, although he accepted a Bible and promised to read it.

Soon after arriving at Port Said we received a reassuring cable from C.M.S. Headquarters to say that our medical and hotel expenses would all be met by the C.M.S. representative in Cairo, and assuring us of the prayers of all the fellowship; cables and letters from home were also a tremendous source of comfort and strength to us at that time.

As Nancy gradually began to regain strength, the question arose of how we were to get home from Port Said. The British Consul was sympathetic and did his best, but berths on board ship were scarce at that time. I vividly recollect accompanying various ship's agents and spending sweltering hours trying to persuade some kindly captain to take us on board his ship. I would gladly have worked my passage in any capacity, but Nancy was still pitifully weak and Anne just a shadow of her former bonny bouncing self. We saw little during that breathlessly hot July in Port Said to endear the place to us, apart from its magnificent sunsets. The drab dusty city seemed far removed from the bright lights and glitter of the dockside, with its famous "Gully Gully men" performing their incredible feats of magic, the cheerful traders and less attractive picture postcard salesmen. Occasionally, I caught the ferry to near-by Port Fuad for a swim, but such diversions were rare and it was with a sense of relief we heard early one morning from the Consulate that a passage had been secured for us on the New Zealand ship S.S. *Rangitata*, due in at midday and sailing the same afternoon.

Just five weeks after our arrival in Port Said, we bade our farewells to the hospital staff and in particular to Dr. Saunders. His parting remark to Nancy was, "Of course, you'll never return to Africa!" to which she replied, "But supposing God brings us back?" To which he could only return a rueful shrug.

The less said about our journey on the *Rangitata*, familiarly known as the "Mangy Tata", the better. The long crowded voyage from New Zealand and Australia had already frayed nerves and tempers, and more than once I was called in to separate wildly shrieking females fighting for the dubious favours of a steward or deck hand.

Nancy's abscess still required daily dressings in the ship's surgery, and her condition was hardly improved by having to share a single berth cabin with five other ladies deep in the bowels of the ship. I had to collect Anne in her pram at six o'clock every morning, before the other occupants of the cabin emerged from their bunks, and then join in the mad rush for a line on which to hang out her nappies.

One gleam of light emerged from an otherwise bleak voyage. One day Nancy noticed a young man reading a Christian book. She enquired if he was a Christian, to which he replied, "No, but a friend of mine on board is doing his best to make me one!" His friend was a likeable young fellow brought up in Chefoo C.I.M. School, who had resisted Christ's claims on his life until, in a Japanese P.O.W. Camp, he began reading his Bible again and was soundly converted! In that huge ship's company we discovered only a handful of Christians but we enjoyed fellowship together and found opportunities for witnessing to a number of people.

As we berthed at Tilbury on the hottest August day for years, a dock strike was in full swing. Our first glimpse of England was thus rather jaundiced, but a warm welcome from our many friends and loved ones soon made us feel at home after an absence of nearly eight years.

10

IT WAS A glorious afternoon with the Lakeland town of Keswick looking its best. The rain and mist had lifted, at least for a few hours, and Derwentwater sparkled in the sunshine.

We had been enjoying a week under canvas in the Y.L.C. Camp run by evangelist Roy Hession. Several of us who had come to know him well and had seen the transformation God had wrought in him the previous Easter at a residential conference in Matlock, were sharing a bell tent together: Joe Church, William Nagenda, Yosiya Kinuka, Lawrence Barham, Peter Guillebaud and myself. I still have a photograph of that group, although I need no such reminder. That week was the culmination of a quite remarkable furlough during which we had been knit together into a team as never before. Invitations poured in for us to go and share news of what the Lord had been doing in Africa, and in addition to an unusually heavy deputation programme we found ourselves travelling together to France, Switzerland and all over England. Everywhere we met with the same hunger and longing for reality. Sometimes we fell into the trap of over-emphasising some particular aspect of the truths which had become so meaningful to us. The Five Steps along which we ourselves had been so clearly led, of Prayerfulness, Brokenness, Openness, Oneness and Fullness had become experimentally very real to each of us. There were, however, indications that they could easily become a technique, a method, a "Ruanda message", which must be slavishly copied—and therein lay danger; a danger which William Nagenda and Yosiya Kinuka were quick to spot and refute. They were visiting England for the first time and right from the beginning were greatly used by God. "Why do you talk so much about revival?" they asked us. "This is a new word to us! Surely in Africa it was Jesus of whom we spoke—Jesus and His precious blood which alone can cleanse from sin." Once William took a large Bible and fixed right in the centre of it a white circle. "For me," he said, "that's JESUS, right in the centre! All that stems from Him—light, fellowship, revival, healing, tongues, even salvation itself radiates out from Him. If once you take any one of those and put that in the centre, JESUS gets out of focus and you begin to get error!" How we praised then, and still do, for the spiritual discernment and wisdom of our African brethren, and how greatly it is needed today.

We had set aside a time in the midst of a very full programme to arrange the details of our proposed transfer from C.M.S. Uganda to the Ruanda Mission. The previous seven years, though outstanding and rewarding in so many ways, had not been easy. Seven years after my ordination I still remained a deacon; a fact which deep down rankled, especially as the hierarchy of the church had expressed in the strongest terms their doubts and fears concerning the whole balokole movement. Even the bishop, while not saying so in as many words, had hinted that in view of Nancy's poor health record it might be as well for us not to return. It was just then that the invitation had come, graciously and lovingly expressed, to join the Ruanda Mission. To be accepted, appreciated, part of a close-knit fellowship again, all seemed so right and obvious. Nothing now remained except to finalise one or two details. We had been joined in a picnic tea on "the Heads" overlooking Derwentwater by Nancy and several wives and others closely involved, who were not actually under canvas in the camp. A very happy party, and yet ... was it imagination or did William and Yosiya seem just a little hesitant?—not quite as certain as the rest of us that this was indeed the Lord's plan for Nancy and me? It soon transpired that they were *not* entirely happy about it, nor it appeared were any of our African brethren in Uganda. But what was it all about? Why hadn't they spoken sooner? Why had they left it so late?

Gradually it all came out. They had hoped so much that we would see it for ourselves, that they wouldn't need to say anything. We hadn't however, so now they felt they must share with us what they had all been feeling. It appeared that Nsibambi, with his remarkable spiritual insight, had been particularly concerned, even posing three questions which he felt we needed to face before the Lord.

The first was "Had God changed our call?" We had always testified to the fact that He had called us to Uganda. Why then were we contemplating leaving Uganda and going to work in Ruanda? There were, of course, ways in which we could rationalise that one! The suggestion had been that we should go to work with Joe at Kabale in Kigezi, which although administered by the Ruanda Mission was technically still in Uganda! But even as we rather lamely uttered the explanation we knew it to be just an excuse. God had never changed our call and we were still as committed as ever to work for Him anywhere He saw fit to send us, even in Uganda.

The second question was harder to swallow. "Does Bill realise," our brethren enquired, "that he is rather like an orange? An orange sitting on a plate may look very nice, but it isn't fulfilling its function unless it is willing to be squeezed!" I had read much the same in Oswald Chambers's challenging book *My Utmost for His Highest*—of grapes that needed to be squeezed if the juice was ever to flow forth, regardless of whose hand does the squeezing—but somehow I had never seen the point. This was a very searching question and Nancy and I had to leave the rest of the party and take a boat out on Derwentwater in order to face up afresh to the whole issue of our will or God's. Tenderly but clearly the Lord revealed to us the wrong motives, the hurt pride, the depths of unbrokenness of which we—especially I—were still so capable, and enabled us to be willing not only to return to Uganda but to be squeezed for Him. Philippians 2; verses 5–11, came alive again, "Let this mind be in you which was also in Christ Jesus..."

It wasn't until the following morning, as we were on our way to the big tent for the Bible Reading, that I remembered there had been three questions, of which so far we had only heard two! What was the third? It proved a surprising one. "Had I ever repented to the Bishop?" "Of what?" I asked. Surely I couldn't repent of the stand taken at Mukono, or of my identification with the balokole, however disapproving those in authority might be of them? No, my brethren explained, it was none of those things—rather surely it was my whole *attitude* of which I needed to repent. The resentment and the injured pride, the hard critical reactions which had gradually, almost imperceptibly, robbed me of Calvary love for those with whom I differed, making me something of an Ishmael to my fellow missionaries and Church authorities. I was reminded of a previous occasion when I took a strong line regarding the location of an evangelist, who I felt was being treated unjustly. Nsibambi had invited me to go and see him and have a chat about the whole situation which was engendering a good deal of heat. I told him, in no uncertain terms what I felt, and was somewhat taken aback when he replied gently that my attitude was so militant, it was difficult to discern what the Lord was trying to say. Could I possibly wait a few days and then meet again?

This time Nsibambi was ready for me! Taking a well-thumbed copy of *Finney's Lectures on Revival* and turning to a certain page he had carefully marked, he asked if I would read aloud the appropriate passage. I have forgotten exactly what it said, but it was to the effect that no matter what the opponents of revival might do, they could never in any way prevent it, but if those seeking to promote revival did so with a wrong spirit then revival would cease. Looking at me with a face aglow with the love of God, Nsibambi repeated, "Wrong spirit, brother Bill, wrong spirit," and I felt rebuked and ashamed. How slow we are to learn our lessons, but how gracious and patient God is in His dealings with us. Just as He had shown years before, through that particular episode, how wrong my attitude had been, so now again, but in a much deeper way, He had to teach me the lesson of brokenness I still find myself so slow to learn.

I wrote that costly letter, asking the Bishop's forgiveness for my wrong attitudes, and all the sting, resentment, and bitterness were swept away. Brokenness really did work! The blood of Jesus really did cleanse and in its place came flooding in a new genuine love, together with a fresh understanding of the great problems which the Bishop faced.

A few weeks later I received a letter from Clifford Martin, our former Vicar and close friend who had since become Bishop of Liverpool, saying how thrilled he was to hear from Bishop Stuart asking if he would priest me by "letters dimissiory" before our return to Africa as he was himself due for leave and would probably just miss me. We had never expected such a gracious gesture but were overjoyed to think that Clifford would be conducting the service. The only question was when it could be fitted into his full programme? He had just one free Sunday available, October 5th. If I could fit that in at such short notice he suggested ordaining me at the parish church of St. Helen's, Lancs., where another mutual friend, Canon Bill Bailey, was Vicar. Entirely unknown to the Bishop, that very weekend had long been booked in my diary for a three-day Mission to the young people of St. Helen's Parish Church, at which my fellow missioners were none other than William Nagenda and Yosiya Kinuka! It was an unforgettable occasion and well worth waiting for. Nancy had found a babysitter for Anne and was able to join me at the Bishop's, and kind friends brought my mother up by road. Bill Bailey acted as Archdeacon, while Philip Ridsdale, a Uganda missionary serving his curacy under him, acted as Bishop's chaplain, and Yosiya was one of those who with the Bishop laid hands on me. The young people among whom we had been conducting special meetings formed the choir. The Africans were so overjoyed that after the service they joined us in the vestry and hugged the Bishop (robes and all) and were duly hugged by him.

We shall never forget that leave. God had so many lessons to teach us, though often we were slow to learn them. It wasn't at all easy having no fixed abode of our own. Nancy's home had been destroyed by a bomb and her mother and eldest sister lived together in a house too small for the three of us. My mother had sold our home when I first went into training ten years previously and shared a tiny cottage with a friend in Wallington. During that leave we moved no fewer than fourteen times; a week or two here, a month there, with Nancy still far from well, with a small baby and without a car!

II

WE COULD SCARCELY credit it. We were actually on our way back to Uganda. This time on the S.S. *Mantola*, a small one-class British India ship, with a comfortable cabin and excellent cuisine. Best of all we were travelling in company with Drs. Harold and Isobel Adeney and their young family, who were returning to Ruanda. Nancy had somehow managed to pass her medicals and Anne was trotting around and chattering away and much more of a handful on board ship than when we came home a little over a year ago. I was grateful for a breathing space in which to take stock and evaluate the new lessons God had been teaching us during that momentous furlough.

We certainly needed such a time, for when we reached Mombasa an unexpected shock awaited us. "You will proceed," read our instructions, "to Iganga where you have been appointed acting Principal of the Teacher Training College." IGANGA!—a notoriously unhealthy mission station in the heart of Busoga, hot, humid and famous for its missionary casualties. Teacher training! I, who had no teaching qualifications whatever and had never trained a teacher in my life ... Was it some kind of joke? How could they do this to us in view of Nancy's health? The resentful, rebellious thoughts raced through our minds as we baked in the oven-like customs sheds at Mombasa, clearing our baggage and preparing for the forty-eight hour railway journey, now so familiar, to Kampala. Even Anne seemed to sense the atmosphere and be less placid and cheerful than usual. Should we ever have offered to return to Uganda where we evidently weren't welcomed or even wanted?

That same evening, however, as the train puffed and panted along, the Lord reminded us of that afternoon at Keswick when He had spoken so clearly and unmistakably to us. "... squeezed oranges!" "... let this mind be in you ..." and once again we began to know His peace.

We met with a warm welcome at Kampala. Was it imagination or were folk more friendly? Certainly a number of them expressed concern, even indignation, regarding our location—to the extent of urging us to demand that it be reconsidered. On the journey, however, the Lord had spoken to us both very clearly about this. "The servant of the Lord must not strive"; this was not "our battle, but the Lord's!"

The next morning, in response to an official summons, I duly reported at the secretarial office to receive confirmation of our posting. "Well, Butler, what do you think about going to Iganga?" I was asked. I cheerfully replied that we were quite happy! This came as a shock as they had evidently anticipated a somewhat different reaction—so much so that it was decided to call a further meeting of the Standing Committee to discuss again where we should go. A few days later we heard that far from being sent to Iganga we had been relocated to Kako, which for ten years had been without a missionary except as a base for Gladys Flack, the Mothers' Union worker. Although we had hitherto not had much to do with

Gladys, we knew her to be a dedicated missionary and one with whom we felt sure we would enjoy immediate fellowship, which certainly proved to be the case. Not only was Kako a far healthier station than Iganga, it was also on the main trunk road crossing the equator *en route* for Ankole, Kigezi and Ruanda! As if this wasn't enough I was designated "District Youth Adviser", thus setting me free at last to do the very job as an evangelist which nine years before I had set out to do but for which I had not been spiritually prepared. So commenced one of the happiest and most fruitful periods of our ministry in Uganda.

We soon discovered Kako to be not only one of the healthiest but loveliest of all Uganda mission stations, with Masaka only eight miles away, where a number of European Government officials lived, and where we could do our weekly shopping. The many African brethren living on or in the vicinity of Kako Hill gave us an enthusiastic welcome, and we quickly settled down in our new environment. An unexpected gift allowed us to purchase a second-hand Chevrolet estate car, in excellent condition, enabling me to arrange a series of evangelistic safaris in the surrounding district with the co-operation and consent of the Rural Dean and other pastors.

The climate of suspicion and opposition to the balokole movement had radically changed, so much so that invitations began pouring in from churches and schools for miles around, and I found myself with a team of African brethren engaged almost non-stop in mission after mission, in which we had the joy of seeing hundreds of men and women, boys and girls, won to the Saviour. It could have been devastatingly lonely for Nancy had it not been for the fellowship she enjoyed with four African teachers living near by, who were responsible for the Girls' Primary School on Kako Hill. They were there as the outcome of a daring experiment in which the supervisor of girls' education in Kampala had deliberately located a team of committed Christian teachers to work together, instead of in scattered ones and twos under difficult and often unsympathetic conditions. The result was apparent for all to see, in a school where Christ was manifestly the Head. Many of the girls responded to the Gospel so clearly presented, and the school became an example of what could be achieved when given the right priorities. The invariable problems still arose of lying, theft and immorality, but the standards set by the Headmistress and her helpers were such that soon parents were clamouring to send their children to a school where they were encouraged to live genuinely Christian lives. Not only the four teachers, but wives of brethren living near by surrounded Nancy with loving, caring fellowship, while Gladys, on her periodic stays at Kako in the midst of her Mothers' Union safaris, was also able to keep a watchful eye on her and Anne, to see that she kept fit and happy during my many absences from home. One wife remarked to Nancy, "Praise the Lord, sister, you're just like one of us; sitting at home looking after the children, while your husband's away on safari!"

In May 1949 Nancy gave birth in Mengo Hospital to our son Andrew William. In view of the difficult time she had after giving birth to Anne she went into Mengo Hospital some weeks early. As riots were in progress she had to be driven majestically into Kampala in an armoured car.

Invitations came from further and further afield until it became necessary to invite William and Yosiya and others to join us in missions and conventions all over Uganda. Although William's licence to preach in church had never been formally restored he was in great demand throughout the country and often over the borders of Kenya, Tanganyika, Ruanda and Burundi and even the Sudan. Later he travelled widely in England, Europe, India and many other countries, exerting a truly remarkable ministry. On one occasion, after we had seen tremendous blessing in various places, we were invited to a mission centre where everything seemed to go wrong. The Mission itself appeared dead and lifeless, nothing was going according to plan and I was growing anxious and frustrated. Yosiya Kinuka to whom, with William, I owe such a debt of love and gratitude took me quietly on one side and asked me why I was losing my peace. "I suppose because everything's going wrong," I answered, to which Yosiya replied, "But why are *you* worrying? After all, you are only the team's chauffeur, aren't you?" I had actually imagined that I was its leader! It was a salutory lesson, one of many, though administered so graciously as to rob it of all offence, and through it I began to learn how to find and accept my place in the team.

I have often been asked what methods we used in expounding the Gospel during those fruitful days. We followed no particular technique; certainly each member of the team knew the Scriptures well, but our preparation usually consisted more of prayer and ensuring that our lines of communication were clear with the Lord and with each other, than any formal preparation or sermon notes. Usually two or three would speak, sometimes as many as four; one beginning with a clear exposition of some passage of Scripture, the others taking up where he left off. The result was immensely powerful. The nail would be hammered relentlessly home, the point clearly made and underlined, often strikingly illustrated with personal testimony, with plenty of opportunity for audience participation in question and answer sessions. We often used a simple visual aid. A blackboard with pin men sketches, for example of Psalm 40; verses 2 and 3: "He brought me up out of the horrible pit and from the miry clay, and set my feet upon a rock. He established my goings and has put a new song into my mouth, even praise unto our God. Many shall see it and fear and shall turn unto the Lord." (cf. *Out of the Pit*, by Dr. J. E. Church.)

An influential chief once attended a mission at which we were using this illustration. He was a notoriously evil man, a heavy drinker, with many concubines, and was suspected of dabbling in witchcraft (although a nominal Christian who had been baptised and confirmed). We were amazed to see him come to church at all but he attended every meeting. One evening, as the crowd was dispersing, he said, "Please pray for me, I am in great need." Later, a few of us drove round to his palatial house. We shared our experience with him, telling how Jesus had delivered us out of various pits of sin, and then suggested a time of prayer. Without any prompting from us he poured out his heart in prayer and penitence, then springing to his feet he said, "Praise God, I too have come out of the pit!" Nothing would satisfy him but to accompany us to the house at which the team was staying; and I shall always remember on our return seeing that dignified figure standing in the light of our car headlamps, telling the rest of the team of his new-found joy and release. The following day was Sunday and many people knelt to greet him as he entered church. "Have you heard the news?" he said. "Last night I was saved!" To another, "Thank God, He has brought me out of the pit!" Later in church he gave his testimony, referring to his many concubines for whom he was making provision and returning to their respective homes, and reinstating his "ring wife" as he described her. He told too of the calabashes of drink which he had poured away and of the witchcraft charms he had burned the night before. We had spoken to him about none of these things, but the Holy Spirit had.

During my leave in England it was suggested that I should take a refresher course in theology. One day my tutor, a gracious and godly man, enquired how we went about presenting the Gospel in Uganda. A trifle pink behind the ears I admitted that we often used simple "line drawings" on the blackboard and at his request enlarged on the "pit" theme. After nearly two hours, to my amazement he exclaimed, "You realise, don't you, this is *profound theology*!" I would not have dared to make such a claim, but it was a great encouragement to hear this pronouncement from the lips of a theologian, himself the author of several scholarly volumes.

The floodgates seemed to open during those three years and although there were still critics of the balokole, more and more were coming to realise that their preaching and teaching was deeply Scriptural and that they were not, as had at first been feared, some divisive breakaway sectarian movement. Indeed, right from the earliest days when pressure was strongest upon the authorities to remove the balokole from the Church, and on the balokole to form a new denomination, God had kept it within the Church—a Church which to a great extent had grown cold and formal and dead, comprising many nominal Christians, but nevertheless still His Church. We began to hear of clergymen and teachers—one here, one there—confessing, sometimes with tears and costly restitution, stolen church money, wrong relationships, acts of immorality. Missionaries began to add their testimonies to the chorus of praise and deliverance; the new song that so many were learning to sing to the English tune of "Glory, glory, alleluia": —

Tukutendereza Yesu
(We praise you Jesus)
Yesu Omwana gw'endiga
(Jesus, thou lamb of God)
Omusaigwo gunazzizza
(Your blood is continually cleansing me)
Nkwebaza, Omulokozi
(I praise you, Saviour)

which became virtually the anthem of revival throughout East Africa.

Those seven years in the "wilderness" of suspicion and scorn, even of persecution, had not been in vain. At last they were beginning to bear fruit in new lives, new understanding of the Gospel and new glorious beginnings.

12

EACH YEAR MISSIONARIES were required to write an annual letter to C.M.S. in London giving an account of activities over the previous twelve months.

I find it fascinating, some twenty-seven years later, to read the report which I sent home in August 1949 to Dr. Max Warren, then General Secretary, as it illustrates some of the new beginnings touched on in the previous chapter.

ANNUAL LETTER 1949

From Rev. and Mrs. W. H. A. Butler C.M.S. KAKO,
P.O. MASAKA,
UGANDA, B.E.A.
August 1949

Dear Dr. Warren,

Once again I must preface our annual letter with thanksgiving for God's great and manifest blessings during the last year.

In Uganda, as you may remember, one of the ways in which we celebrated the C.M.S. 3rd Jubilee, was by holding special district missions throughout the Protectorate. In my last letter, I described in some detail the missions that took place here in Buddu where I am engaged in evangelistic and pastoral work. Since then, in addition to my normal work, it has been my privilege to take part, usually with a team of keen Africans, in similar missions in the districts of Bulemezi, Toro and Bunyoro; and at Buloba Girls' School, Kings' College, Budo, and Mwiri College, Busoga.

These missions like others held throughout the country have met with the most encouraging response, resulting in many definite conversions, and in the deepening and strengthening of spiritual life of many others. One of their marked features has been the solid (though I trust not too heavy) teaching of scriptural truths, with special emphasis on such fundamental subjects as sin, salvation and growth in the Christian life. Another interesting point has been the absence of any frothy emotionalism, which so often is attributed to revival movements. Not least has this been evident in the work among young people; notably at Budo during the mission recently held there, when over forty senior boys and girls accepted Christ as their personal Saviour, without any pressure of "hand-raising" or outward excitement whatever. From Gayaza, the biggest girls' school in Uganda, comes news only last week of a remarkable wave of blessing in which many girls have been saved—again without any accompanying hysteria or excitement—also from the Alliance High School in Kenya where a similar remarkable work is taking place.

It has been a great joy to see the way in which, with very few exceptions, so many recently converted folk have been going on quietly and steadily with their Lord; often in the teeth of bitter opposition; sometimes, in the case of the younger ones, in spite of actual persecution from parents or guardians; even to the extent of being thrown out of their homes. I need hardly add how much such "new born babes" need prayer backing and support both from us out here, and from those at home who are praying for God's work in Africa.

Another great cause for thanksgiving is the way in which the "balokole controversy" seems to be dying down and the church beginning to use their fire and zeal for the extension of Christ's Kingdom; while the balokole for their part are gladly co-operating with the leaders of the church. It seems that at last, the fact is being realised and accepted, that the balokole have never intended, and never do intend to leave their church, and the result of this acceptance is seen in the access of new life and vigour to the Church of Uganda which can only bring glory to God.

Our Missionary Retreat and Conference this year were also memorable for the way in which the Lord dealt with us as a mission. We were convicted of coldness and lack of love and burdened for these to whom we have been sent. We were brought to realise too how often our reserve and shyness brought barriers between one and another; and few who were present will ever forget Colonel Grimshaw's stirring challenge to us, who have been redeemed by the precious blood of Christ, to enter into a "free, holy, unfettered fellowship" with God and with each other.

Your book *Truth of Vision* which we had studied previously, individually and in small groups, provided a challenging and inspiring basis for the talks and discussions which followed, and the resultant note of reality and high resolve which characterised the whole Retreat and Conference afforded a welcome relief to the dark background of rioting and disturbances into which at that time Buganda was being plunged.

I am more than ever convinced that the only lasting

solution to the acute and growing problems of Uganda, spiritual, social and political, is to be found in the true revival of the Church. In so far as this has been and is taking place, such problems as racial discrimination, communism, materialism, etc., pale into insignificance. It should be noted that of all the many nominal Christians, and even clergy who were so unfortunately associated with the "Bataka" (the subversive political party responsible for the riots) not one of the balokole could be found.

At the government hospital in the neighbouring township of Masaka—the second largest hospital in Uganda—there are ten saved nurses, and the head hospital orderly is also an outstanding Christian. In the post office, out of a staff of about eight Africans, the chief telegram linesman, and his three senior assistants, are all keen, and "key" men! The government officials who come into touch with such people, whether in hospital or in post office, cannot speak too highly of them or of their work; and their lives are a constant glowing testimony to the saving and keeping power of Jesus Christ.

I should like at this point to give some brief sketches of some of the outstanding memories of the past year to illustrate what the Lord is doing in these days of opportunity in Uganda.

For a long time it seemed as if only the "poor and the halt and the lame and the blind" were among those who were being affected by the revival; but during the past year or so, a number of more influential people—among them chiefs and clergy—have also been converted. Some months ago, the wife of a grand old ex-chief died. Both she and her husband had been saved about four years previously and it had made just all the difference to their married life and home. Such a funeral affords wonderful opportunities for testimony and witness, and the revived Africans have been given such victory over fear of death that now, as one of them recently remarked to me "you hardly know whether the 'Brethren' are going to a funeral or a wedding or a christening; all are such joyful occasions!" (that reminds me of a certain missionary at one such funeral, who had a dear old woman turn to him with a beaming face and say, "Oh, Bwana, just you wait till *you* die, we'll give you such a *lovely* funeral!")—but at the same time, they show amazing love and sympathy to the bereaved. On this particular occasion, there must have been between five and six hundred people present, including the Prime Minister of Buganda and other prominent men. It was wonderful to see the old man get up, and stand by the grave of his wife with whom he had spent over forty years, and testify that in the midst of his sorrow at his loss, he had tremendous joy in his heart because he knew she had gone to be with Jesus, and that soon he would be joining her.

I remember another funeral—perhaps the most victorious I've ever taken. The two-year-old child of a great friend of mine, a pastor, had been crushed to death in his arms the previous day in a lorry smash. The parents, both saved, were simply radiant, and I shall never forget my friend, whose own arm had been broken in the smash saying: "Yesterday I was in a lorry with my wife and children, and our youngest son in my arms. Then the lorry crashed and overturned and our little one woke up to find himself in the arms of Jesus!" Can it be wondered that in the light of such victory revival is spreading?

Another picture comes to mind: a visit to a village church among some very primitive cattle folk in this district, where wonderful things have been happening, and hundreds—whole kraals at a time—of these simple ignorant peasant folk are being gloriously saved. It was thrilling to be surrounded by hundreds of them, many rather smelly and distinctly dirty but just full of thanksgiving to God because they have been saved from their sin and fear and superstition. I nearly had an accident there though! After a typical morning's service (which included morning prayer, two sermons, Holy Communion, and seven babies to baptise, taking over three hours in all) we all went outside and sat under a sort of banana leaf canopy which they had erected specially for the occasion for us all to sit together. I cheerfully dipped my "matoke"—a sticky yellow mass of cooked plantain, looking not unlike plasticine, but tasting much nicer—into the accompanying sauce which is always provided; not realising that, being cattle folk, it consisted of nothing less than pure melted goat's fat! I managed to get down two or three mouthfuls, and then had to "freeze" or else I'd surely have been sick on the spot! They were all most concerned at my lack of appetite.

Services out in the villages are most enjoyable, even if they lack something of the reverence and order to which we are accustomed at home, or in our central churches out here. They often begin an hour or more after the scheduled time, and there are plenty of distractions during the service itself. The "choir" may break down completely after making three or four false starts in leading an unfamiliar tune; a hen or a dog may stroll in and dispute the possession of reading desk or pulpit with whoever is taking the service; or one of the children who have to sit—or sleep—through these interminable services may cause a diversion by falling asleep and banging his or her head on the hard mud dung-smeared floor.

This latter fact makes us all the more anxious to get Sunday School and children's work really going, not only in a few central churches, or where there happen to be Europeans to run and supervise them, but throughout the whole church, and in every village church as well. This is bound to take time, and meanwhile we have been encouraged by progress already made in this direction. We had a very worthwhile three-day course for prospective Sunday School teachers here last December, when nearly a hundred came into Kako, and heard talks and lectures and demonstrations, and took part in very lively discussions on methods of children's work. We have been making increasing use of flannelgraphs this tour, and have found this method of visual aid exceedingly valuable not only for children, but for adults as well! During Holy Week, we took a series of flannelgraph talks entitled "Guideposts to the Cross" which were followed with breathless interest by a packed congregation. Miss Gladys Flack, who is also stationed at Kako, and who is responsible for all the Mothers' Union and women's work in Uganda, has brought back with her a film-strip projector which she very kindly lends me from time to time, which is also greatly appreciated, though I am inclined to think that on the whole, flannelgraphs, besides being very much cheaper, are more suited to the average audience that one meets with in Uganda.

A few weeks ago, we returned home from Kampala, where, on May 24th, my wife gave birth to our second child, Andrew William. Unfortunately the girl who helps Nancy with our little daughter was unable to return with us, owing to herself being ill, and we rather wondered how we were going to manage, as I was due to go on safari almost immediately after we got home. We needn't have worried, for after the usual welcome, we were touched by the arrival of a deputation of teachers from the girls' school, asking to be allowed to take over the jobs which our "ayah" would normally have done, including washing and ironing the nappies, bathing Anne, etc. . . . It may seem quite a small thing, but it is typical of the loving thought and fellowship in which we are so rich here in Uganda.

In closing, I am reproducing a letter which came a few weeks ago to my wife, from one of our African friends —Anne's godmother actually—which serves yet further to illustrate how simple, but how real is the faith of our African brethren:

My dear Nancy,

I meant to write to you on Saturday but I had a lot to be done so I lost time to write. How are you and dear Anne? I hope you are all well and praising. Praise the Lord for all He is doing at Kako and elsewhere. He is helping us here too. We had a nice church service this morning. God has spoken to us how He loves and cares for us; how Jesus finds us everywhere we are, where Satan takes us, and He brings us back on His shoulder very lovingly, and He has showed us we must be like little children. A little child doesn't mind how dirty he is when he wants to be lifted up by his mother or father. He only comes with all his dirt, and lifts his arms, and cries for help. He doesn't count how clean you are, but because he loves you, he only comes to you as he is. You lift him and cleanse him. That is how we must go to Jesus for help. We must not be grown-ups, as you know they know how dirty they are, and don't want to be seen in rags. How I wish to be like a little girl, and sit always on Jesus's shoulder!

Another African, trying to explain what the phrase "cleansed in the blood of Jesus" really meant, thought for a few moments, and then said with a beaming smile: "It's like the wind-screen wiper you have on your car window; you just switch on the wiper, and it keeps on cleansing away the dirt, so that the window is always clean and transparent, and that's just what Jesus wants to do to our hearts!"

Well, this is a long letter, and it is high time it was finished. It comes again with warm personal wishes to yourself, and your fellow Secretaries, and with grateful thanks for all the prayer and fellowship of the home staff.

Yours very sincerely,
Bill and Nancy Butler

13

WE HAD BEEN hearing reports for some time of the hunger for God's word, among the cattle-loving people of Mawogola, between Buganda and the plains of Ankole, and of how they wanted a team to come and visit them, sitting where they sat amid the mud, manure and flies, and just gossiping the Gospel. Some had actually never seen a white man, and one had never visited them in their kraals. Somehow we felt the Lord constraining us to go, and an extract from a diary letter written to my mother describes that week:

Saturday, January 21st, 1950 Left early for Kampala with a car-load of brethren to conduct a wedding for three couples in the cathedral. A very happy occasion, at which I was supported by Disani Mukasa and Benoni Kagwa. A huge crowd had gathered, some from over a hundred miles away, not because those getting married were anybody particular, but just because they were the Lord's children, and all wanted to share in their joy. The testimonies at the joint reception afterwards were grand; not least that of the "Namasole"—the Queen Mother—who was converted only last year. She got up with her face simply beaming, and said, "You know, all of you, that I've only recently begun walking in this way of salvation, but I'm determined to go on in it right to the very end, for it's such a *satisfying* way!"

We got away about six p.m. and I took two of the "couples" to Kabungo for their honeymoon, getting home about nine thirty p.m. (183 miles altogether).

Sunday, January 22nd Set out for Mawogola, the cattle district of Buddu, where the nomadic Balalo herd their cows. Picked up Musajakawa and two saved Balalo brethren *en route*, and got to the local chief's house in time for a welcome cup of tea. Found that the bikes which were to have been left there for us had been left nine miles further on; which involved a further nine miles of almost impossible going for the poor old bus! The "road" was literally just rain gulleys washed out of the scrub; but by dint of crawling along at about eight m.p.h. we managed to reach the appointed place without any great damage being done, except that the car was boiling furiously, and one spring was badly cracked.

We found the bikes awaiting us, and transferred our bedding and camp kit to them and set off for the first kraal. It was interesting to see how they manage along footpaths no more than a foot wide; often down precipitous slopes; also most illuminating to see how they never cycle uphill, even so much as a couple of yards. At once, they're off, and shoving the bike up, on foot! Being brethren, they took wonderful care of me, and wouldn't allow me to take any of the luggage on the back of my bike—sharing the extra load out among themselves. The amount each was able to carry was quite phenomenal. It's not at all unusual to see a man cycling along with a woman grasping a child and bundle, sitting perched on the back of his bike!

About six p.m. we arrived at the kraal where we were to stay. Practically all its members had been converted.

It is quite remarkable. Men, women and children have just accepted the Gospel in all its simplicity, and their lives are utterly transformed as a result. The kraal itself of course, and their manner of life, i.e. herding cows, goes on exactly as before, as it has done for countless generations; but the difference in their behaviour is incredible. They gave us such a welcome! These cattle people are quite primitive, living a life entirely apart from the average African. They are cattle herders, pure and simple, of Hamitic descent. Tall, with thin aquiline features, and very aristocratic, they have their own language, which covers the whole of East Africa, whatever may be the tribal language of the area into which they have wandered. Cows, especially before Balalo are saved, are the be-all and end-all of life to them. They literally live and die by their cattle, existing communally in bee-hive huts, which can be put up in the space of a couple of hours or so, simply consisting of bent sticks over which grass is thrown, with a small opening about two feet high and one and a half feet wide. The average time a kraal remains in one place is two or three months. Sometimes, during the dry weather, when in search of water for their cows, they may move as often as once a month. When this happens, the whole kraal, men, women and children migrate five or six miles—sometimes more—and by evening the kraal will be complete again; each hut in its appointed place, with its huge encircling thorn bush hedge, ten feet high or more. The cows are all brought in each evening (the kraal I was staying in was quite a small one, with a population of about eighty folk, and three to five hundred cows)—and stand in the middle. Their milk provides all the human inhabitants with their normal diet; though occasionally if a cow dies or has to be killed they will eat meat. They make butter in gourds, by the simple process of swinging the gourd round and round for an hour or more until the thick milk sets. This they sell in local markets. They also sometimes supplement their diet by drinking the cow's blood.

To return to our arrival. The whole community turned out to greet us and so did the flies in their thousands! I've never seen so many in my life, though I was assured that it was nothing to what they can be like in May or June, then we were led to the hut they had prepared for us. It was beautifully clean and sweet inside, with fresh-cut grass on the floor, and due to the small opening cool and dark, so that we ceased being plagued with flies as soon as we got inside. Musajakawa and I soon had our safari beds made up and then tea—thick and very sweet, made entirely with milk!—was brought to us. Afterwards, we were taken round the whole kraal, and formally taken into every hut, so that we had the freedom of the kraal. Each hut is circular, and about half the circumference of an ordinary army bell-tent, and only four to five feet high. (Ours, being specially built for us, was a little larger.) In these a family of as many as six or seven people live and move and have their being! These dear folk, realising that we would find it difficult to cope with nothing but milk (Musajakawa is a Muganda clergyman, nearly as far removed from Balalo as Europeans), had transported on foot, and by bike, enough "matoke"—the plantain, staple diet of Buganda, which I always eat when on safari—to keep us going all the time we were their guests. They had also killed a cow in our honour, so that we had plenty of meat and gravy with which to eat our "matoke".

That evening, we sat out under a tropical sky with stars blazing overhead, and had a fellowship meeting. It is amazing how quickly and deeply they have grown in spiritual knowledge. Many of them are still unable to read or write. All of them were living, right up to the day of their conversion, in darkest paganism, of which adultery, drunkenness and witchcraft were the norm, and yet here was a whole kraal—full of transformed people—whose very faces shone with joy; where drink, adultery and immorality are just not known any longer. All this, mark you, without any direct missionary influence whatever. Simply the result of the testimonies of a handful of their own people who heard the Gospel five or six years ago and were saved. It was a very moving experience to spend these days with them, and one for which I can only praise the Lord.

Monday, January 23rd Woke early; had a big meal of "matoke", and then set out before the sun got too hot, for a neighbouring pagan kraal, about eight miles away. Again, we followed "rain-gulley" tracks, on our bikes; seeing traces of lion and other wild game as we went. Hence the need for a high thornbush fence all round each kraal! We arrived dripping with perspiration at our destination, after about two hours of gruelling travel. What a contrast! Their kraal was exactly the same in its general appearance, except that it was far, far dirtier, with cow dung everywhere and flies even worse than at Nyakatabo—but it was in the darkness of their faces, and the atmosphere of sin and degradation, that one chiefly realised the amazing difference Jesus Christ has brought into the lives of those who have heard of and trusted Him. They seemed genuinely eager to hear our message for, having seen the difference in their neighbours, they wanted to hear what we had to say. The whole kraal therefore—a rather bigger one than the balokole one we had just left, with the exception of just a handful of children told to go off and herd the cows—gathered together under a huge tree, over ninety feet high. Two of us spoke, very very simply, being translated from Luganda into their own language. They listened intently for nearly two hours with hardly a movement. It was my first experience of preaching the Gospel to absolute raw pagans, and I couldn't help wondering how much was penetrating! You can judge my amazement when at the end of the preaching, without any "appeal" or emotionalism whatever, an elderly woman and a young man said they were saved! It was so unexpected, but beyond any shadow of doubt they were, there and then, "born again". "Old things had passed away, behold all things had become new." Their very faces showed the difference, and by evening, the young man, without a word from us, had cut off and burned his witchcraft charms which he had worn since the day of his birth! (It was interesting in this connection, how many of the saved Balalo have told us in their own words, that even when they knew nothing whatever about the Gospel, "the very name of Jesus sounded sweet to our ears".) The brethren that we took over with us from Nyakatabo were thrilled with what had happened at Lwachende—the pagan kraal—and felt sure the Lord had begun a real work in their midst. We were unable to stay there, much as we would love to have done, as they were just about to move to fresh watering places, and had stayed on an extra day, simply in order to welcome us. We therefore returned the same evening—having eaten nothing since breakfast!—to Nyakatabo.

Tuesday, January 24th Up early again, and had the

whole morning with the Nyakatabo folk. Real solid Bible teaching, illustrated from personal testimony. Felt it was a deep and blessed time. Had a final meal there, then set out about three p.m. by bikes again for where we had left the car on Sunday, reaching it two hours later, finding all safe and sound. Got to Kikoma, the church built by the balokole belonging to the two kraals of which Zabuloni and Kosiya are the respective Headmen, at about six-thirty p.m. Again met with a great welcome from the brethren, a number of whom have come in from their outlying kraals in order to look after us and give us hospitality!

Wednesday, January 25th Travelled in the car to the big fortnightly market—more like an English "Fair"—held at Sembabule, six miles or so from Kikoma. It was a most interesting experience to see such a market. There were dozens of stalls of different kinds; some for food, others for beer and various drinks; some for fetishes and charms. There were also great enclosures where cattle were bought and sold. The whole fair covered quite a large area. We went as a team, with our "merchandise"—the Gospel! After thoroughly surveying the ground, we chose as our "pulpit" an enormous ant-hill over fifteen feet high, from which we could see and be seen by most of the folk on the fair ground. I started off, taking Isaiah 55; verses 1 and 2 as our theme, "Ho, everyone that is thirsty ... come and drink ..." A big crowd gathered, and listened very well, considering the noise that surrounded us. Cattle lowing, vendors crying their wares, drummers banging away at their dancing drums, etc.... Two of the brethren also spoke, very simply but clearly. We then spent several hours doing personal work, and talking with interested individuals. In the afternoon, we went along a rather better track than that of last Sunday, to Zabuloni's kraal, bigger than I've yet seen, and had a lovely time with the brethren there; getting back to Kikoma in time for the evening meal, and an early bed (sleeping in the little mud church this time, but very comfortable).

Thursday, January 26th A very good turnout indeed from the neighbouring kraals, to Kikoma church, which was just packed with almost as many outside as there were in. Three of us spoke, using the flannelgraph, taking the picture of the Serpents in the Wilderness. We spent all morning, and made it a real teaching time, as most of those present were from Zabuloni's and Kosiya's kraals, and were truly converted, just needing building up. It was a grand time, and there was a testimony meeting outside afterwards. Quite impromptu and informal, but very real, and full of life. Several confessed to having grown cold and to "playing with snakes" in their lives, by allowing sins of various kinds, but they were rejoicing at the fresh realisation of the victory of Calvary, and the power of the precious blood of the Lord Jesus Christ to cleanse from all sin.

Had a lovely fellowship meal together at midday, and then baptised three of the brethren's babes. A really joyful occasion. Packed up the car at three p.m. and set out for home, only thirty miles or so away. Got home about tea time, full of praise to the Lord for this very inspiring safari among the cattle folk. Truly, He does delight still to "choose the weak things of the world, and things that are not ... that no flesh shall glory in His presence".

14

THIS TIME IT was my turn for the doctor. A severe headache, rigors, high temperature, the lot. A few days earlier I had returned from the safari just described among the nomadic cattle folk on the plains of Mawogola.

I rattled along in a ramshackle old ambulance on the eighty mile journey to Mengo hospital in Kampala. The medical officer had been sent for from our nearest township, Masaka, and diagnosed a severe attack of typhoid. This was the devil's counter-attack. Weeks later, still in Mengo hospital after seemingly endless tests and unremitting fever, it transpired that it wasn't typhoid after all but brucellosis or "undulant fever", obviously contracted from milk drunk in the kraals which, in spite of all precautions, had not been adequately boiled.

Meanwhile back at home Nancy was wrestling with another problem. We had been planning to hold a convention at Kako to which over a thousand delegates were expected from all over East Africa, including many missionaries and a party from England, Switzerland—even as far afield as India! The African brethren were tremendous. They were helping in every possible way but even so looked to Nancy for a lead, and as usual she rose magnificently to the occasion.

Then Andrew fell ill. Anne and he loved Kako; it was so quiet and peaceful on top of that lovely hill, overlooking Lake Nabugabo, with Lake Victoria shimmering in the distant heat haze. Andrew kept remarkably fit on the whole, apart from odd childish complaints, but this was different. He was running a high temperature and evidently felt pretty sick. Again the medical officer had to be sent for and again he thought it might be typhoid. "By the way, Mrs. Butler," he said, as he was about to leave, "what's all this I hear about some sort of gathering you propose holding here? I am afraid it's out of the question. I must forbid it."

Nancy thought he was joking but it soon became evident that he was very much in earnest and that, if he had his way, the whole idea of a convention would have to be scrapped. Ignoring the fact that I was not after all suffering from typhoid, nor was Andrew, who within a day or two was perfectly fit again, the D.M.O. maintained that it was impossible on health grounds to arrange for a thousand or more people to be adequately housed, fed and watered for nearly a week on a mission station which, apart from various day schools, normally housed only ourselves and a missionary colleague. Admittedly we too had shared the same forebodings, especially in view of the growing numbers of missionaries and other Europeans who had written to say they were coming. First twenty, then forty, then seventy; eventually more than twice that number! Where and how were they all to be housed and fed? Nor was this the only problem; I was still eighty miles away in hospital and Nancy was having to cope with one crisis after another on her own. And yet, of course, she was not alone. As Corrie Ten Boom loves to say, "God has no problems, only plans!" As Nancy sat there quietly before the Lord a pattern began to emerge. She thought of Dr. Theo Goodchild in charge of our Mission Hospital at Mengo, who was doing everything possible to get me back on my feet again in time for the convention. Could he use his influence to get the medical embargo lifted? A message was phoned through to him via the Masaka post office, eight miles away. The telephone men were brethren and in daily touch with Kampala! Sure enough, he was able to persuade the Senior Medical Officer to pay a visit to Kako and inspect the site himself, after which it needed only a quiet word with his over-zealous junior to resolve the seemingly insoluble problem. Permission was granted. The convention could be held.

Lieutenant Colonel George Grimshaw had recently arrived in Uganda as C.M.S. Regional Representative and had been blessed by what he had seen of revival in East Africa. At a convention in Kenya soon after his arrival, his name was added to the list of speakers, not under his usual title but simply as "Glumshaw"! And as "Brother Glumshaw" we shall always gratefully remember him. As soon as he heard of our difficulties in finding suitable extra accommodation he got in touch with the Commanding Officer of the King's African Rifles who kindly lent us a dining marquee and forms seating over two hundred, and sufficient bell-tents to sleep all our extra guests; even supplying us with lorries and army personnel to put up and dismantle the tents and mount a guard on them during the meetings. Our African brethren worked magnificently, digging innumerable latrine pits, transforming classrooms into dormitories and collecting the food required to feed such a multitude. One problem remained, that of water. The school buildings had several large tanks in which to collect rainwater off the galvanised iron roofs, but permission could only be given to use it if we guaranteed to fill every tank again in time for the new term which started the week after the convention. Realising that this might mean having to fill tanks at great expense and with enormous effort from the swamps if no rain fell (and this was the dry season) we, of course, had to agree to the conditions. The very hour after the big marquee and other tents were dismantled the heavens opened in a tremendous deluge, with every tank on Kako Hill, including our own, overflowing—one of the many miracles God wrought for us that remarkable week.

Three weeks before the convention I was released from hospital and although still feeling weak and wobbly, was able to return home in time to relieve Nancy of some of the burden. A missionary friend of ours, Kathleen Mawer, a trained dietitian and caterer, was free to come early and organise the entire cooking and catering for our 150 European and various distinguished guests, including the Kabaka's mother, and the Princess Lucy Rubuga from Toro. The same friend was able to advise us over the number of empty four-gallon paraffin tins needed to boil the drinking water for such a large company. Peter Guillebaud built a hot-water system with old petrol drums which provided us with an ample supply of hot water. A band of helpers was found to assist our cook in preparing the meals. A lorry brought and manned by our friends from Namutamba proved invaluable in ferrying people, food and firewood. It was so wonderful once we let God take control, to see everything run so peacefully and smoothly. Even Andrew's unexpected illness had brought out into the open the issue of health and hygiene, which otherwise might not have been raised until it was too late. The government health inspectors sent out from

Masaka to ensure that everything was being done to maintain good hygiene were frankly amazed. There was no litter, no mess, no adverse report, only the highest praise for the cleanliness and spotless condition of the camp! Police had been alerted to possible trouble in view of the variety of tribes attending the convention, but were astonished at the way everybody mingled so happily without a single political "incident". The army, too, could hardly believe their ears when they heard the throng of willing helpers joyfully singing as they helped to erect the large marquee and subsidiary tents, remarking that they were more used to swearing and cursing accompanying such chores, than the praises of Jesus!

None of us who attended that convention will ever forget it. Although there have been many far larger gatherings, these were hand-picked delegates from virtually every tribe in East Africa. Cars, lorries and buses came rolling continuously up Kako Hill, each overflowing with eager, expectant delegates. From Kenya, from Tanganyika, from Ruanda, Burundi and the Congo, even from the Sudan they came. The large bat-ridden church in Kako was packed to the doors with as many outside as in, listening through loudspeakers powered by relays of car batteries.

The theme of the whole convention was "The prisoner set free". Joe Church started off with a simple blackboard drawing of a man sitting despairingly in the condemned cell, awaiting execution. Hanging on the wall was a list of all the crimes and offences he had committed, for any one of which he deserved to die. It was a vivid picture of sinful man, awaiting judgment, hopeless and helpless, unable to do anything to free himself. Speaker after speaker followed, enlarging and elaborating on the theme, "the wages of sin is death". The Holy Spirit was deeply at work in the hearts of many, Europeans as well as Africans. The talks were all interpreted fluently and with power into either Luganda or English, while others sat together in small groups and heard the message in their own language or dialect.

One of the outstanding memories of Kako convention, however, was not the preaching, powerful and effective as that undoubtedly was, but the remarkable sense of fellowship and freedom we all enjoyed together. This was especially evident towards the end of each day when, all over the hill, various groups met together after the evening meal to share how God had been dealing with them. Rarely had such profound testimonies been heard. Missionaries acknowledging as sin their criticism, jealousy, bitterness, resentment, impurity and anger, lack of vision and love for each other and for those among whom they had come to minister. Africans repenting of deep rooted fear, suspicion and mistrust of Europeans, of tribal differences and hatred. As the masks were stripped off and each of us faced the reality of his own sinfulness, there was no need for unhealthy introspection or despair. The Holy Spirit was convincing us of sin, righteousness and judgment, and as the Bible so clearly reminds us we found there was indeed no difference: "All have sinned and come short of the Glory of God." This reminds me of a phrase I shall always treasure in a farewell speech made just before we left Uganda: "We love our brother Bill because although the colour of his skin is white, we know his heart is as black as ours!"

For the final meeting we had invited the Rural Dean of Kako to give the blessing. A godfearing upright man, rather reserved and austere, he lacked any assurance of salvation. Once when we had been camping out together in an empty schoolroom, after talking until late into the night, he seemed deeply moved and acknowledged the fact that he was "a hell-deserving sinner". On being urged to accept Christ as his personal Saviour he replied, "No, don't rush me! I want time to think this through." That was three months before. We had an outstanding closing message brought to us by Roy Hession, one of the party who had flown out from England to join us. We saw the Lord Jesus taking our place on the Cross, His precious blood flowing to redeem and cleanse the foulest sinner and set the prisoner free. We saw the captive released from prison, rejoicing in a wonderful salvation purchased at such a price.

As we were singing the concluding hymn the Rural Dean whispered to me, "Will you please interpret into English for me, I have something I want to say!" My faith was weak. I feared he might say something which would lessen the impact, or confuse the issue which had been made so clear.

"We have seen that man in prison," he said quietly. "I have been like a warder, keeping people locked up in jail . . . It is because I had never seen clearly how to get out of prison myself, but today I have come to see, and I myself have come out of that prison and I hope that many others will follow me!"

A moment of almost incredulous silence. I was weeping; I could hardly believe it. Then a great burst of praise and thanksgiving, "*TUKUTENDEREZA YESU*"! as it had never before been sung in that church! Quietly the Rural Dean lifted his hand for silence. After pronouncing the blessing, he began to walk towards the church door. I can't remember such joy—joy over a repentant Rural

Dean! He was hugged so often that his ribs must have nearly cracked. Then his wife was saved; we had never before seen her smile, but now she was beaming from ear to ear, and singing the praises of her new found Saviour! The local chief was next; then in one rejoicing little band after another we heard of prisoners being released and set free. It was an unforgettable sight—a hill ablaze for God!

15

THAT WAS NOT the end of the story—rather it was the beginning of an exciting and continuing chapter which is still being written.

Revival has sometimes been likened to a forest fire; one patch catching alight, and in turn igniting another. Kako Convention was like that. Although numerically small, for similar gatherings had attracted three or four times as many, it consisted of carefully picked delegates from all over East Africa, themselves spiritual leaders in the areas from which they came. As they returned rejoicing and on fire, others caught alight, smouldering embers kindled into flame, and reports began to come in from all over East Africa of individuals and churches being revived.

Such blessing could hardly go unchallenged. Even while we were at Kako we heard whispers among some of our brethren from Kenya of a sinister secret society, later known as Mau Mau, which involved the taking of hideous oaths and ceremonies and resulting in the martyrdom of many outstanding African Christians. It seemed as if God had been preparing them for what lay ahead, this time the testing fire of persecution, hatred and bitterness, out of which emerged, phoenix-like, a church purified and renewed. Canon Cecil Bewes, a missionary in Kenya for many years who revisited that country at the height of the Mau Mau troubles, wrote:

> This is the most thrilling fellowship that ever I met in my life, a fellowship that surpasses all the barriers of colour and race. Africans have confessed that they used to hate Europeans until they came to know them as brothers in Christ. Europeans are finding a new joy and oneness with Africans and have had to repent of their former attitude of superiority and pride. A Kikuyu pastor writes, "there is no colour at the Cross, likewise there is no colourbar at the Cross". Great conventions have been held at Kako and elsewhere, where African and Englishman together shared the cooking, the water carrying and the wood chopping, as well as the preaching; shared too in the joy of welcoming into the family one after another who came to know Christ as Saviour. It was not for nothing that the Kikuyu Church was recalled—just in time—to a new emphasis on the precious blood of Jesus as the only hope of salvation. The revival has made it real for some of us all over again, for we can see in it our only hope, our only ground for confidence. The Mau Mau were trusting in the blood of a pagan sacrifice, the Christian Kikuyu find the perfect answer in the precious blood of Jesus, shed once for all on Calvary but ever flowing free, ever available for cleansing and pardon and peace.

Later the Church in the Sudan experienced the agonies of civil war. It was my privilege in 1974 to take part in a Pastors' Conference in Juba attended by over two hundred pastors and evangelists, reunited for the first time in seventeen years, where I had the joy of meeting several whom I had first encountered at Kako, and who testified to the way it had prepared them for the tragic days which lay ahead.

The Rev. John Collinson, describing the impact on him of those early days of revival in Africa, wrote a little leaflet from which, with his permission, I quote the following extracts ...

Sometimes it is asked what we mean by Brokenness. Brokenness is not easy to define but can be clearly seen in the reactions of Jesus, especially as He approached the Cross and His crucifixion. I think it can be applied personally in this way:

When to do the will of God means that even my Christian Brethren will not understand, and I remember that "Neither did His brethren believe in Him" (John 7 : 5), and I bow my head to obey and accept the misunderstanding, THIS IS BROKENNESS.

When I am misrepresented or deliberately misinterpreted, and I remember that Jesus was falsely accused but He "held His peace", and I bow my head to accept the accusation without trying to justify myself, THIS IS BROKENNESS.

When another is preferred before me and I am deliberately passed over, and I remember that they cried "Away with this man, and release unto us Barabbas", (Luke 23 : 18) and I bow my head and accept rejection, THIS IS BROKENNESS.

My plans are brushed aside and I see the work of years brought to ruins by the ambitions of others and I remember that Jesus allowed them to lead Him away to crucify Him (Matthew 27 : 31), and He accepted that place of failure and I bow my head and accept the injustice without bitterness, THIS IS BROKENNESS.

When in order to be right with my God it is necessary to take the humbling path of confession and restitution, and I remember that Jesus "made Himself of no reputation" and "humbled Himself ... unto death, even the death of the Cross" (Philippians 2 : 8), and I bow my head and am ready to accept the shame of exposure, THIS IS BROKENNESS.

When others take unfair advantage of my being a Christian and treat my belongings as public property, and I remember "they stripped Him", and "parted His garments, casting lots" (Matthew 27 : 28, 35), and I bow my head and accept "joyfully the spoiling of my goods" for His sake, THIS IS BROKENNESS.

When one acts towards me in an unforgiveable way, and I remember that when He was crucified Jesus prayed "Father, forgive them; for they know not what they do" (Luke 23 : 34), and I bow my head and accept any behaviour towards me as permitted by my loving Father, THIS IS BROKENNESS.

When people expect the impossible of me and more than time or human strength can give, I remember that Jesus said, "This is my body which is given for you ..." (Luke 22 : 19), and I repent of my self-indulgence and lack of self-giving for others, THIS IS BROKENNESS.

Roy Hession in his widely-read book *Calvary Road*[1] writes:

> Brokenness, however, is but the beginning of revival. Revival itself is being absolutely filled to overflowing with the Holy Spirit, and that is victorious living. If we were asked this moment if we were filled with the Holy Spirit, how many of us would dare to answer "Yes"? Revival is when we can say "yes" at any moment of the day. It is not egoistic to say so, for filling to overflowing is utterly and completely God's work—it is all of grace. All we have to do is to present our empty, broken self and let Him fill and keep us filled. Andrew Murray says, "Just as water ever seeks and fills the lowest place, so the moment God finds you abased and empty, His glory and power flow in." The picture that has made things simple and clear to so many of us is that of the human heart as a cup which we hold out to Jesus, longing that He may fill it with the Water of Life. Jesus is pictured as bearing the golden water-pot with the Water of Life. As He passes by, He looks into our cup, and if it is clean He fills it to overflowing with the Water of Life; and as Jesus is always passing by, the cup can be always running over. That is something of what David meant when he said, "My cup runneth over". This is revival—the constant peace of God ruling in our hearts because we are full to overflowing with blessing ourselves, and sharing it with others. People imagine that dying to self makes one miserable, but it is just the opposite. It is the refusal to die to self that makes

1. Published by Christian Literature Crusade.

one miserable. The more we know of death with Him, the more we shall know of His life in us, and so the more of real peace and joy. His life, too, will overflow through us to lost souls in a real concern for their salvation, and to our fellow Christians in a deep desire for their blessing.

Only one thing prevents Jesus filling our cups as He passes by, and that is sin in one of its thousand forms. The Lord Jesus does not fill dirty cups. Anything that springs from self, however small it may be, is sin. Self-effort or self-complacency in service is sin. Self-pity in trials or difficulties, self-seeking in business or Christian work, self-indulgence in one's spare time, sensitiveness, touchiness, resentment and self-defence when we are hurt or injured by others, self-consciousness, reserve, worry, fear, all spring from self and all are sin and make our cups unclean. But all of them were put into that other cup, which the Lord Jesus shrank from momentarily in Gethsemane, but which He drank to the dregs at Calvary—the cup of our sin; and if we will allow Him to show us what is in our cups and then give it Him, He will cleanse them in the precious blood that still flows for sin. That does not mean mere cleansing from the guilt of sin, but from the stain and pollution of it, so that we have "no more conscience of sin" there. And as He cleanses our cups, so He fills them to overflowing with His Holy Spirit.

In Ruanda and Burundi, where the flame of revival first began to burn so brightly over forty years ago, deep-rooted tribal differences have resulted in traumatic situations, culminating in 1972 in the appalling "happenings" in Burundi in which thousands lost their lives. Even there, where so many outstanding leaders have been lost to the Church, there are widows in whom one can find no trace of bitterness or hatred, and young people discovering the warmth of love and unity that can only be found in Jesus Christ.

Many of the inspired leaders of those early days are now in Heaven. Others, spiritually very much alive, have grown physically old and inactive, but God has never allowed the fires of revival to burn out completely. Bishop Lawrence Barham loved to tell of the earthenware pots in which Africans kept their smouldering ashes. Sometimes the pot would appear cold and lifeless, but as its owner blew on the seemingly dead embers, they soon glowed, until they burst once more into flame.

No one who attended the 1974 Lausanne Congress on Evangelism will ever forget Bishop Festo Kivengere's inspired visual aid, when having testified to the way God is still working in his country Uganda, he invited all his brethren from East Africa to join him on the platform where, with radiant faces, they sang the glory song, "*Tukutendereza Yesu!*" In his message at the service of Holy Communion with which that great gathering concluded, and with which this chapter too must end. Festo had this to say:

"The Cross is God's eternal love reaching out and embracing a broken humanity in its mighty embrace.

"Because sin entered history, man was turned in the direction of death instead of life, in the direction of darkness instead of light. He became, not what God made him to be, but a disintegrated person, hating himself, hating the world, hating other men.

"Man's cry of despair entered into the heart of God, stirred eternity and God responded, for God so loved the world that He gave His beloved Son. The beloved Son came one hundred per cent of the way to where man was, took His place beside him, and put His blessed hand over his trembling hand. Hope had entered humanity.

"God addressed himself to the deepest human need. What is it? It is deep-seated human guilt. This is the shattering experience of men everywhere, no matter whether you cover it up with long psychological words or theological expressions or sociological understandings. It is still there. You dress me up, you make me fat physically. I still am a suffering man unless you deal with my guilt. I will commit suicide in my suit or my loincloth.

"The Cross goes deep into my deterioration. It is not superficial. And there is no despair in Calvary, no need it cannot meet. It deals with my hostilities, restores my relationships with God and my neighbour.

"I was converted under men who were almost illiterate, but when they talked about hell, they wept, and when they talked about Heaven, they laughed. When they talked about the Cross and the needs of a sinner, I saw it portrayed in their lives and faces.

"One day before I was converted, it was my duty as a teacher to speak to the entire school in chapel, but I had nothing to say. My young brother, nine years old, stepped out in front of these 250 boys, took his New Testament and preached Jesus Christ crucified. For twenty-five minutes you could have heard a pin drop. I was absolutely taken aback. When he finished, ten boys got up and accepted the Lord. The secret was the

Cross. Then, as God breathes through the Cross upon men, they become evangelists.

"They also suffer. A little man in my particular part of the world stood before a chief and gave his testimony. For that he was beaten until he fell down. He got up with a shining face and said, 'I have not yet resisted unto blood, fighting against sin.' He did not realise that blood was streaming out of his nostrils. He was a man inspired by the love of Calvary.

"The Cross is the price of paying for my sin and yours. It cost God that. And it costs every man. It will cost you blood and sweat. There is no cheap Gospel anywhere. Let us therefore take account, accept the love that God gave, and let the Cross do all its work in us and through us to the world."

MISSIONARY CLASSICS IN HODDER CHRISTIAN PAPERBACKS

DR. VIGGO OLSEN

Daktar: Diplomat in Bangladesh

The powerful, enthralling story of a brilliant young doctor and his incredible hardships, and the way God seemed to move heaven and earth to answer his people's needs.

"In the tradition of David Livingstone"—

New York Times

ALFRED BOSSHARDT

The Guiding Hand

Captivity and answered prayer in China

Alfred Bosshardt was taken prisoner by the Communists, in whose hands he remained for twenty months of the Long March through China. His story is one of faith and endurance under the most demoralising conditions.

"I expected to read of miraculous deliverances, but instead he was merely sustained and strengthened in the situation. It was all so real"—

Crusade

DOROTHY CLARKE-WILSON

Ten Fingers for God

"A fascinating record of the life of Paul Brand, the distinguished orthopaedic surgeon, who has pioneered as a bone specialist in the surgical treatment of the hands and feet of leprosy patients . . . a notable book"—

Expository Times

"A really marvellous story of patience and expertise"—

Guardian